MW01127062

HOW TO READ PEOPLE LIKE A BOOK

The Complete Guide to Speed-Reading People, Understand Body Language, Decode Intentions, and Connect Effortlessly

Written By

JASON MILLER

COPYRIGHT © 2020 BY JASON MILLER

All rights reserved. No part of this book may be reproduced or used in any manner without the written permission of the copyright owner except for the use of quotations in a book review.

Illustrations copyright © 2020 by Ralph Williams

Cover photography by Ralph Williams

First Edition: November 2020

Produced by Jason Miller

Printed in the United States of America

Table of Contents

Part - I

Part – II

INTRODUCTION

H ave you ever looked at those people who show up at a seemingly boring event or a party and suddenly, their presence makes the whole place come alive? Do you know at least one person who seems to be at the center of every circle but somehow manages to be gracious and attentive to every person that they come across? Would you want to become this kind of person? If you answered yes to any of these questions, this book, "How to Read People Like a Book; the Complete Guide to Speed-reading People, Understanding Body Language, Decode Intentions and Connect Effortlessly" might hold the key to helping you develop social skills relevant for the successful building of relationships. The two-part series that come together to make this book merges two sides of a coin; understanding the intricate nature of people and learning how to effectively interact with them. This successful merger simplifies the difficult aspects of relating with people and makes you more adept at communication.

You see, man is a social creature. We were made to commune with each other. However, many of us find ourselves struggling with this fundamental biological need. We find it difficult to get past our inner insecurities, our negative perceptions which we project to the world and we struggle with the basic foundations of starting and building healthy relationships. And even though these negative emotions, perceptions and experience reside in our thoughts most of the time, we subconsciously show them in our body language and verbal communications. We identify with our insecurities more than our strengths and this plays out in the way we deal with people. The inability to correctly analyze a person's words and actions will see you thrusting your negativity into the situation and ruining any chances you might have with this person long before you conclude the exchange of greetings. Regardless of whether those relationships are for business, pleasure or strictly familial, it is important to understand the nature of the person you are dealing with. You have to learn the social ability to mirror their actions in order to get a more positive outcome and then push past your fears to enable you to find the courage to take things to the next level.

This book addresses those critical fears that have gone on to carve out your attitudes towards relationships. Many of us have lost wonderful relationships with long-term potential because we feel that we need time to get to know people and then accept them into our space. Here's a newsflash for you; in the world of speed dating, social media and profile swiping, by the time you feel comfortable enough to get to know a person intimately before making a decision to form a relationship with them, you will have lost them. Using some of the techniques employed by profilers in leading intelligence agencies like the FBI and CIA, the guidelines laid out in this book enables you to shorten your regular people vetting process by helping you focus on those important details that significantly shines a light on the true character behind the person you are evaluating and helps you make snap decisions as to whether to pursue that relationship or not. Apart from that, you would also learn how to;

- Initiate conversations at the drop of a hat and keep the people you are talking with interested and engaged

- Let go those crazy lies you tell yourself that might be negatively affecting your relationships

- Correctly identify physical and verbal cues people give off through their body language and learn to separate real friends from fake friends

- Become more confident in your verbal and nonverbal communication skills regardless of the environment you find yourself in

- Build and add value to your social network by growing your inner circle strategically

Besides looking into your immediate social environment and reading the clues in that setting, another important thing you have to understand is how to strategically position yourself in a way that makes it easier for people to talk to. You may apply all of the observatory skills you will learn here in a social setting but still fail to present yourself as someone people want to be friends with. "How to Read People Like a Book; the Complete Guide to SpeedReading People, Understanding Body Language, Decode Intentions and Connect Effortlessly" is a book that helps you look inward when it comes to connecting with people.

The book is a two-part series that starts out with a detailed guide on How to Analyze People in an everyday life before giving you practical lessons on How to Talk to Strangers, connect with them and make a proper first impression. The information provided in both books will highlight critical aspects of your social life that require additional improvements. Find out those things that stand in the way of you building long lasting relationships that are healthy and capitalize on the social strengths that you have.

A lot of books that promise to help you become more successful socially tend to be one-sided. They either focus on building you up internally or teaching you how to manipulate people in your circle. This is not one of those books. Here, you get a wholesome narrative on what really happens in social settings. And beyond that, you will also learn how to sieve through the emotional mush that clouds our judgement because you also get insider trade secrets on how the minds of people really work and how certain subconscious behavioral cues may reveal their hidden agenda. Wouldn't you want to know what a person might be intending even before they take action? The thing is, you don't need to be a mind reader to get that kind of power. All you need to do is grab a copy of this book, turn over to the next page and start taking the necessary steps that would lead you to your social objective. It may be scary at first but it is going to be a fun transformation I promise. So, what are you waiting for? Let us get started!!!

$Part - I$

THE ART OF ANALYZING PEOPLE

How to Master the Art of Analyzing and Influencing Anyone with Body Language, Covert NLP, Emotional Intelligence and Ethical Manipulation

Chapter 1

What's the Problem? – How to Analyze People Instantly Using Proven and Successful Techniques

B y reading people, we don't mean that you have to read their minds like a psychic. Instead, you have to analyze their gestures and expressions to calculate what they actually mean. Reading people is about sensing their intentions like what is running in their heads through their behavior. If you gain this ability, you will be able to ameliorate your intimate and social life. When you have read and understood people, you can easily tailor your way of communication to suit their state of mind. This is how you can make an impact in a conversation.

Read People: Who They Really Are. How to Unmask Someone?

The best way to read people is not to let your emotions get over you. Forget about your past experiences. If you are trying to judge people by your past experiences, you will likely misread them. Pay detailed attention to their dressing. If they are wearing casual dresses like t-shirts and jeans, they like to be comfortable, so if they prefer comfort over hardness, they are unlikely to work hard and grow in a competitive environment. Also, see if they are wearing any pendants or stones. If they do, this indicates their spiritual inclination. This helps you judge in a better way.

Another important thing to take into consideration is a person's posture. A high head posture tells us that the person in question is highly confident. If he or she cowers, they suffer from low esteem.

In addition, the emotions that appear on a person's face tell a lot about it. Deep frown lines on a person's forehead suggest that the person is prone to overthinking. Similarly, if a person has pursed lips, he is most likely in anger and is harboring feelings of contempt. If he is grinding his teeth or has a clenched jaw, this means that he is tense.

Most people don't like to get involved in small talk. It is justified given the magnitude of our daily workload and the preoccupation associated with it. But if you ponder over it for a moment, you will realize that small talk, in fact, offers you a great opportunity to get familiarity with a stranger. You can read how he is going to behave in certain situations. That's how you are able to detect any abnormal behavior.

The Way You Treat or React to Other People Depends on the Way You Analyze Them

Once you have read people, it can greatly help you form your reaction to their questions or behavior. For example, if you have deduced that a person is highly confident and social, you will have to set your tone and posture to match his style. If he is confident but you are cowering, you two cannot have a healthy and productive conversation or collaboration.

Similarly, if a person has pursed lips, she is not in a position to listen to anything productive that you throw in her way because she is perturbed by something and will remain inattentive during a conversation. A person will only attentively listen to what you are saying if you are talking according to his or her mental state. If he is cowering and you are head high, he will feel intimidated by your posture and will not be able to open up his heart in front of you. The conversation is likely to end inconclusively or in a deadlock.

How Can You Be Accurate in Reading Someone Using Human Psychology, Body Language, and Personality Traits?

If you want to read people by means of their body language, you have to take a look at the cues that they share with each other with their gestures. Our face is one of the body parts that have considerable importance. Then comes body proxemics. This includes how your body tends to move in space. The third most important thing is body ornaments like your clothes and the jewelry you wear. Firstly, you need to decode a person's cues like interpreting the information that is hidden in their emotions and personality.

Look to Their Eyes

When it comes to reading other people's language, their eyes can be really helpful. You have to pay attention to their eye-contact and how they tend to look away while talking. If they exhibit the tendency to avoid direct eye contact, this indicates that they are not enjoying your small talk or serious discussion. In addition, this indicates disinterest and also deceit in some cases. You can also sense deceit if a person looks away or to the sides. If the person is looking down instead of looking straight, it means he is nervous. In some cases, it also shows submissiveness.

The blinking rate is also important when it comes to reading people's minds. Blinking rate increases when a person is stressed. When a person is touching his face during blinking, he might be lying to you. If the person is glancing at something, this suggests that he has a deep desire for that very thing. Similarly, glancing at a person suggests that the person desires to meet him or her or wants to talk to him or her. If he is glancing at the door, he desires to leave.

If a person, who you are talking to, is looking to the right and upwards, he might be lying to you. If he is looking to the left and upwards, he is speaking the truth. The reason is that it is natural for people to look to the left and upwards when they are using imagination. (Scott, n.d)

Study the Head Movement

The head movement of the person is also of great importance. If the other person is nodding his head when you are talking to him, it either means their patience or lack of patience. If the frequency of nodding is higher than usual, it is the indication that the person is fed up with listening to your talking and needs respite. If she is tilting her head to the sides, she is interested in your talking, but if the tilting is toward the backside, this indicates that the other person is suspicious or uncertain. (Scott, n.d)

Study the Feet

If a person is careful about his nonverbal signals, there is still one fragile point in which you can study to read what is running inside his brain. Why people miss out on controlling their feet is because they are too much focused on keeping in check their facial expressions and other verbal actions. Naturally, a person points his feet while standing or sitting toward the direction in which he wants to go. If he is pointing his feet toward you, he harbors a favorable opinion of you. If you are in a group discussion and a person whom you are talking to is pointing his feet toward some other person instead of you, this is a fair indication that he wants to talk to that person. One important thing is that feet movement and cues are meant to bypass other nonverbal cues. So, even if his facial expressions and eyes say otherwise, you have to follow the cues you pick by his feet.

How Can You Avoid Manipulation by Reading Someone's Mind?

Manipulators have one objective and that is to achieve their goals at any cost. So, their foremost weapon is using deceptive body language. There are some signs that people use when they are emotionally weak and are talking to stressors. But if this is not the case, they are very likely manipulating you by showing exactly the same signs. They will generally use these gestures to gain sympathy from you. Let's roll on to see what these gestures are and how can you avoid manipulation by reading them accurately.

They Will Rub Their Neck and Hands

When a person is manipulating you, he will rub his hands. This most likely indicates self-serving plotting. On the other hand, if he tends to rub his neck, this also signifies the same thing. The manipulator tries to gain your sympathy through this act.

They Will Stroke Their ARMS

When a person is rubbing or scratching his arms, he might have the full intention of manipulating you. This one is tricky because it is possible that the person has other reasons for scratching his arms such as hives. If scratching of arms comes in combination with neck rubbing, this may very likely be a sign of manipulation.

They Will Tap Their Feet

Manipulators tend to shift and tap their feet. This tapping and frequent shifting of feet indicate that they are impatient or even offended. Their impatience will compel you to make a decision in a rush that may most likely not be in your best interest. (English, 2019).

Chapter 2

How Many People Are Gifted with the Talent to Read People Instantly?

Reading people can be a god gifted ability and you can look for certain signs that show that you have that ability wired in your brain. Upon meeting a person for the first time, you usually have a powerful gut feeling which you just cannot explain in a rational way. You instantly form an opinion whether you like them or not. And, over time, when you get to know their real self, you realize that your gut feeling was right. People cannot always explain how they were able to judge others. It is something in their sub-conscious.

Another feeling that most people have but they cannot express is the power to know other people's thoughts. This also is a natural ability. More than once you might have noticed that you were able to tell what other people had on their minds. For example, you bring up a particular topic and leave your friend wondering because he was thinking about bringing up the same topic under discussion.

Sometimes you can accurately tell if your friend is upset. You don't have to communicate with them to know that. It is just his facial expressions that you have to study in order to reach a conclusion. If you are good at this, you have this talent as a god gift.

Some people really boast of their gut feelings. They are pretty sure of escaping dangerous situations just by following their gut feeling. You might have followed your gut and saved yourself from a dangerous situation. For example, your friends are planning a trip to a lake. You cancel the plan at the nick of the time and later find out that all your friends got injured in a road accident. Have you ever had that feeling?

Some people are naturally blessed with the power to detect if someone is lying to them or not. They can tell if someone is twisting the truth or is modifying it. Perhaps they fabricate a story for their personal gains at the cost of your benefit but they don't know that you are pretty good at finding out the loopholes in their stories. Their eyes, lips and hands tell you if they are telling the truth or not.

All the above incidents are pretty common to most of us. Everyone has a particular gift to use when he is caught in a difficult situation, but most people are unable to explain its words. It remains in their subconscious throughout their lives. If you are a Sherlock Holmes fan, you can understand exactly what I want to tell you. (How To Read People Like the FBI, 2018.)

Can Anyone Learn How to Analyze People?

The ability to read people is concerned with their gestures and other nonverbal signs coupled with their words. Well, it is a fact that you can have this ability in your genes, but this is something that can be easily learned. You have to memorize different signs to accurately judge what other people have on their minds. This includes studying, memorizing and then using a person's posture, gestures, voice tone, facial expressions and also the willingness for an eye-contact in the middle of conversations. There is no rule to read people because people are different. Some have mastered the art of becoming a conman while others appear to be wearing their hearts on their sleeves. You can easily tell what they are thinking and what will be their next step? (How To Read People Like the FBI, 2018.)

Some Tricks to Learn to Read People

It is impossible that you may understand the exact thoughts of a person, but it is always possible to read how they are acting. With the help of some psychology tricks, you will be able to learn how to read people.

Objectivity

The first lesson for a learner is to be objective. You must not let your emotions and biases cloud your judgment about a person. If you have already put that person in a kind of stereotype box, you are the least likely to be right about them. Think like a neutral person.

Try to Find out the Normal Behavior of That Person

When you are trying to judge a person, you should look out for his or her normal behavior. Sometimes you miss out on correctly judging a person just because the behavior he is exhibiting is his normal behavior. This can be scratching of arms, rubbing his hands or neck, tapping the feet and looking sideways. All these gestures, we have discussed earlier, pertains to some kind of nonverbal cues, but they can be a part of a person's normal behavior. That's why you need to set a baseline for that. Calculate what is normal and what is not. Biting nails can be common with a person and cannot always be a sign of lying. If you overanalyze, you can misread people and damage your relationship with that person. Scrape this gesture and look out for some other sign that crosses the baseline that you have set for that person's behavior. (How To Read People Like the FBI, 2018.)

Are you sensing any kind of inconsistency in that person's normal behavior and body language? If you are finding inconsistency in their behavior, phoneme can greatly help you reach the right conclusion. A phoneme is a basic unit of phonetics. If the person is lying to you or feeling nervous while talking to you, she will have an inconsistent voice tone. The pith in her voice will raise or lower down while she uses particular words. She can overemphasize some words to make you believe them. At this point, you are being manipulated.

You also need to understand the context behind the speech and gestures. For example, if a person is sitting with arms crossed, it can be a sign of unhappiness. But the person's choice of taking up this posture can be due to decreasing temperature in the room. Also, you should take into account the type of furniture the person is sitting on. If the chair has no arms, then the person will naturally cross his arms to rest them. When you are in the learning phase, you should broaden your field of focus. Focusing on just one body sign will land you in confusion, and you will misjudge the other person. (How To Read People Like the FBI,

2018.)

Trust Your Gut

Last but not least is that you need to trust your gut. Pay close heed to make sense of your emotions as well as feelings. You can tell that by studying how you feel when you meet them. (How To Read People Like the FBI, 2018.)

Is It Enough to Depend on Your Instincts When Analyzing People?

Whenever we are caught up in a difficult situation, we are repeatedly told and also we tell ourselves to trust the gut. This can be a bad situation or a bad person who we think is bent on doing harm to us. The gut factor jumps in to take its toll on our nerves. But for some people, gut feeling is so powerful that they think there is no need for reading people and analyzing body language. (Chu, 2017).

A single incident, a new employee, a new boss or a new job send the wheels spinning in our heads as we try to figure out how they will impact our lives. One reason behind this immense popularity of our gut feeling is that it is a simple answer to some complex questions that keep us awake at night. Answer to all questions is: "Trust your gut."

Let me explain and clear the confusion. Our instincts are not like a magic spell. We say a phrase and things start happening or an airy creature shows itself and fills us in about a particular incident or person. Instinctual feelings or intuition are linked to our past experiences and knowledge. The reason why people have different intuitional powers is that their experiences are different. The unconscious part of our brain starts working immediately after we encounter something new. It is like pattern matching. When we see a person smiling in front of us, our brain will match this sight with loads of data that is stored in our subconscious. Then it goes on to draw a conclusion. The process is so fast that the conscious side of the brain is totally unaware of this process. That's how we receive guidance in certain situations when we feel ourselves in danger. From this, we can deduce that if the experiences and knowledge are of greater size, our instincts work better. (Chu, 2017).

It is not enough to rely on your gut to reach a decision on whether the person is good or bad. What if you misjudge a person's intentions? When you realize his real nature, it will be too late. Take the example of a cop who, by nature of his duty, has to make fast decisions. He doesn't have enough time to scan through detailed information before he acts. So, one misjudgment can take the life of an innocent person. So, if we base our decisions only on our gut feeling, we are likely to end up making the wrong decision that could land us in trouble. The verdict is that you have to pair up gut feeling with the knowledge that you have about reading their gestures.

It is not always a good idea to follow your gut. Sometimes it is better to just eliminate the need for your gut feeling. You can do this by befriending someone and talking to them without heeding to your gut feeling. Your judgment ought to be calculated and well measured, and should be free of certain prejudices. Otherwise, you are highly likely to make a mistake and lose a friend. (Chu, 2017).

What Can You Do to Improve That Skill?

You can predict what others are thinking. You can read their minds, theorize what they are thinking and also understand their gestures. From all the data, you can know their intentions and analyze their emotions. On the basis of this knowledge, you can predict what their beliefs are and what is inside their hearts. All this makes your conversation with that person fun and productive. To achieve this feat, you should focus on brushing up your skills of reading people. Let's see how to do that.

• You need to stay focused and also be present in the current moment. Never think about yourself amid the process.

• You must be all ears to others. Listen to them attentively. Read between the lines, try to understand the context of their speech. Also, try to understand what they are not saying and keeping back. First, process their words in your brain and try to deduce their meaning. After that, you can respond.

• While you are communicating, you ought to study his facial features, his dressing, the jewelry and makeup in case of a female. Don't forget to take a look at his or her hair cut. In addition, you should take into consideration the surroundings where you are communicating with that person. To improve your reading skills you have to be efficient when it comes to studying that person's facial features and dressing. You have to invigorate your observation skills. You should not miss out on anything minute to large. Even a slight aberration in the person's hairstyle should click your brain.

• You should not lose focus due to some intrusive thoughts. Keep it on the person in front of you. Detect any nuance in their behavior and follow how it develops.

• To improve the skill of reading people, you need to stay calm. If something is perturbing you and you are not at peace with yourself, you will not be able to read the person in front of you accurately. Inner calm is directly proportional to focus. The higher the level of your inner calm, the greater your focus will be.

• If you are the kind of person who loses patience too soon, you are least likely to read and analyze other people effectively. Sometimes you have to listen to another person's blabber on end in order to get to know them better. Practice it if you lack this ability.

Chapter 3

Discuss the Different Types of People and How They Fit in the Social Circle.

All of us are full of different flaws that make us feel ashamed. We do have strengths that we want to brag about in front of everyone. Some of us prefer to stay natural in their everyday life while others love to take up their favorite persona to get through different hurdles in their lives. Some people like to make their way by deception, lies and manipulation while others prefer to face stumbling blocks but refuse to deviate from the right path. Whatever our choice of being a person in our lives is, the goal mustn't be of hiding our weaknesses as well as dark spots if we have any. We must allow our flaws to be a part of our personality. We should celebrate our flaws. This is what being human is about. When a person takes up a fake persona, he forgets that the people, who are loving him, are actually loving that persona that he has taken up and not that person who is in hiding under the fake personality. The real success is that people start loving us because of what we are and not because of what we are trying to become.

The Joker

The first category is a joker. The foremost feeling on hearing the word joker is of a person who is cracking jokes and laughing his heart out even during sober conversations. Jokers love jokes, costumes and makeup. Each makeover gives them a new look and personality. They love to hide their real looks and nature to others. Generally, jokers are considered harmless but if we bring to mind batman's joker, things get totally different. A scary and nutty person comes to mind who is evil personified. That joker is always bent on inflicting the greatest pain on the people surrounding him. Can you think of a person who fulfills the above personality traits? Do you know anyone who laughs too much, always cracks jokes or tries to tease others while laughing it out? Beware! Jokers are masters of disguise.

The Smart One

Smart people have the ability to mold themselves according to the situation. They learn or are naturally gifted to adapt to changing circumstances. Smart people always remember to read other people's styles to gain more knowledge about them. They tend to see through the motives behind their acts and also their hidden desires to work with them and gain benefits. Smart people are good at conveying their messages through in an effective manner and without making the slightest buzz. They know how to express their feelings in a clear way, which is the most important thing when it comes to building and strengthening a relationship.

Similarly, smart people are very successful in their businesses or jobs. They work hard to learn how to read people and the rest gets automatically easy for you. You can tell if a person is smart by looking at how they behave with you and other people around him. One important point to note is that smart people are very good at taking care of their personal interests, even at the cost of others.

The Worker

Workers are the people who belong to a specific social class that is known for doing jobs for low pay only to live hand to mouth in their lives. The jobs they do low demand skills and labor and also have low literacy requirements. This category of people also lives off on social welfare programs. Working-class people mostly remain preoccupied with their day-to-day expenditures. They don't have time to take up different personas and disguises. Also, they are not smart enough to get a job done in the easiest way possible. Their brains are generally wired to do it the hard way. These people generally wear their hearts on their sleeves. They are easy to predict and are simple to understand.

The Loyal

These people are hard to find but exist. They are reliable as well as truthful. If a person is loyal to you, he shares affection with you and will not leave you when life gets hard for you. Loyal people think from their hearts and always work for the benefit of the people who are close to them. Just like the working class, loyal people are easily predictable and trustworthy.

The Strong

Physically strong people generally have happy temperament. A strong person has higher levels of physical and mental strength. They don't have self-pity; that's why they are confident and good at judging people and dealing with them. Before they judge other people, they try to judge themselves. In addition, they have higher levels of self-restraint. Their nerves are powerful that's why they are patient. They also are good listeners and observers. Their physical and mental strengths make them very good at reading other people and reaching an educated judgment. They don't hesitate to ask for help when they are in need, and also, they are open to helping others.

Different Types of Personalities

People are driven by their nature when they do this or that and leave you wondering why they did something that looked unwanted to you. It is perfectly normal if you think you need to want to understand someone a bit more than you already do. This someone can be a loved one or a person at our workplace. We have to accept the reality that people are not perfect. We are different and it is this difference and diversity that makes this world a colorful and interesting place to live in. When people stay true to their role, they tend to contribute their bit to this diverse world. Just imagine if we were all created in the same way, how the world look would like then. It would be boring.

Take an example of diversity. When a car hits a motorbike in a road accident, a huge number of people gather at the site. Most of them are on-lookers who are just investigating what happened. Some mourn the wounds of the injured while some call the ambulance. Only a handful of them step up and actually help the injured recover their senses. They try to administer to the first aid and take care of them until the ambulance arrives at the site. It is not that those people leap into a house on fire without thinking about their lives. We react differently to different situations. These reactions are triggered by our fears and desires. Sometimes they motivate us while at other times, they just demotivate us.

In analyzing people, you should know the people around you. What they do and how they react to different situations. By knowing their personality types and the fears that guide their behavior, you can improve how you interact with different people. It helps you read people in a more efficient way so that your interaction with them becomes smooth and your analysis of people broadens and deepens. In addition, you can track down your own personality traits as well as faults. Let's roll on and take a look at different types of people in the world.

The Reformer / Idealist

The Reformer is a perfectionist. They have principles and are conscientious. These kinds of people have certain ideals to follow and they come down hard on themselves as well as on other people. They just love to keep them at pretty high standards. They are dedicated and responsible besides having perfect self-discipline.

They are usually successful in life because they tend to get lots of things to happen in a short span of time, and that too in the right way. They are always looking forward to setting themselves on the right path by eliminating their weaknesses. (9 Personality

Types – Enneagram Numbers, n.d)

The Performer

As the title suggests, these kinds of people will always be setting goals for themselves. They are highly target-oriented individuals and they believe in doing rather than sitting on the couch and thinking day and night. They are always striving for success. This drive makes them pretty excellent at doing things right. You can find them in a big company, a shop or on the street selling vegetables or fruit. Wherever they are, their eyes are always on the horizon. They have dreams of success and they are in the world to make them happen. These kinds of people are considered as role-models by many other people.

They have their fears that drive them toward the top. What makes them perfect is their urge to become somebody. The fear of dying as nobody makes them state-conscious. Instead of discouraging others, they respect the opinion of other people. (9 Personality Types – Enneagram Numbers, n.d)

The Observer

This kind of people spend time on thinking and are of an introvert type. Their focus always is on gaining knowledge. They also prefer reading their own personality instead of reading others. They remain absorbed in themselves and love to play with different types of concepts. They usually abhor worldly attractions like big mansions, cars and social status. They are always busy in searching for themselves. They prefer to observe what is happening in their brains. You can see that these people will lock themselves in their rooms for hours as they love to understand how things go on. This exclusive behavior allows them to concentrate on what they do, that's why they are usually considered as experts on what they do. As they don't have the social skills that are needed to keep relationships healthy, they get overlooked most of the time.

The Adventurer

These kinds of people are fun-loving people. You will see them engaged in enjoyable pursuits and also, they are often in an upbeat mood. They thrive on pleasure and adventures, which makes them a really positive person. They tend to avoid negativity at all costs, which helps them fight off pessimism and stress really well. They are also very optimistic and don't let tough challenges mar their optimism. They are the ones who always find that silver lining in dark clouds. They stick to that silver lining and turn negative situations really fast and really well. (9 Personality Types – Enneagram Numbers, n.d)

Also, they are highly inconsistent. As they are fun-oriented, they remain in a certain work until the fun factor is alive but shoot out of it once they are bored no matter if the work is complete or not. Completion of projects poses a big challenge to them; that's why they struggle to be successful in the practical world.

The Warrior

As the name suggests, these kinds of people love to throw and take the gauntlet. They are strong and have dominating personalities. You can say they are born leaders and are really confident. They are real alphas. They hate to depend on other people and also don't like to reveal their weaknesses. Instead, they use their strengths to give a cover to those people who are around them as their family and friends. They are always ready to take charge of any situation no matter how thundering and dreadful it is. They love to be the masters of their own fate and they also prefer to take control of people as well as circumstances.

Their inner strength also makes them rigid, straight forward and sometimes haughty and harsh. They cannot tolerate signs of weakness in other people. They are ready to confront others on petty issues. They are always ready to express their anger and frustration on things they don't meet up with their expectations. These are the ones that are quite difficult to understand. Their nature is too intense and volatile to let others read them. (9 Personality Types – Enneagram Numbers, n.d).

Chapter 4

Basic but Proven Effective Techniques for Analyzing People

T his chapter will walk you through some basic techniques for analyzing people. You will learn what body signs you have to read in order to understand what is running in the other person's mind. In addition, I will explain in detail the importance of gut feeling and the role it plays when you are trying to read other people. The chapter will also walk you through the importance of emotional energy in reading people.

I have touched upon the topic of studying body signs in the first chapter. This chapter will help you learn in detail what each body sign tells about a person.

Posture

How we carry our bodies speak volumes about our personality and mindset. The posture that we keep our bodies in tells a lot. I have earlier on explained what a straight posture indicates. I am going to add on to the previous information. When observing a person's posture, you should observe whether a person has an open posture or a closed one.

An open posture is when a person keeps the trunk of her body exposed. If you observe it in a person, she is likely to be friendly, willing and open to you. On the other hand, a closed posture is the one in which a person hides the trunk of her body. For example, she will hunch forward or keep her arms crossed. This is the opposite of openness, and the person in question will exhibit hostility and anxiety.

Body Language

Body language is the nonverbal signals that we send through our gestures. In simple words, it is about communication through our bodies. It includes our hand movements and facial expressions to as little things as our pupils. If we observe closely, we will see that people tend to give away a great volume of information through nonverbal signals. As I have already suggested, the key to reading nonverbal signs accurately is to take these signals and study them as a group.

The Eyes

Our eyes are considered as windows to our souls. They are the easiest to learn and most people can do that even without prior training. They tend to reveal a great amount of information about what is running inside our hearts. What we feel or think comes into our eyes. Even a naïve person can take the hint in the eyes of the speaker. But it is not just the eyes that should be studied. Pupils are also very important to know other person's minds. Look out for dilated pupils as they indicate increased cognitive struggle.

Pupils tend to dilate if they are looking at something they appreciate. This is not an easy job to do. If you keep observing different people, you will finally learn how to observe and detect any change in the pupils. If pupils are highly dilated than normal, it means that a person is attracted to someone and is aroused.

Hands, Legs and Arms

Gestures by hands, legs and arms are very important. I'll add on to the previously stated details. Gestures, like our eyes, carry plenty of information about our personalities. Our waving, tapping and pointing have hidden meanings that ought to be understood if you want to master the art of analyzing people. Well, it is important to sort out these gestures as some are cultural traditions like a raised straight palm. In some Asian countries, this suggests hello and in the United States, a thumbs up suggest that everything is fine. You have to keep in view these signs so that they are not mixed up with nonverbal cues.

Coming back to nonverbal cues. If a person has a clenched fist, this indicates anger but, in some cases, this also indicates solidarity especially when shown by a politician or a public figure. For a clear analysis, you should study this gesture combining it with facial expressions and speech. Similarly, in some countries, people use the okay gesture that is formed by touching the index finger with the thumb. In some countries, this suggests that everything is going on fine while in parts of Europe, this means that you are nothing. In some Asian and South American countries, this gesture is considered vulgar.

Arms and legs are also quite useful in nonverbal communication. If a person tends to open his arms and keep it that way, he is an attention seeker and full of life. We have learned earlier on that crossed arms suggest closeness and defensiveness. A common gesture that you might have come across is the one in which a person stands with his or her hands on the hips. This is an indication that the person is fully in charge of circumstances and is ready to face anything. In rare cases, it may suggest aggression.

If a person clasps his hands behind the back, he is bored and anxious about something. We have learned earlier on what tapping our feet means. Besides, tapping your fingers also means a lot. It can be a sign of boredom or frustration. When a person crosses his legs, he is closing off on society and wants some personal space. He will prefer privacy than socialization.

Personal Space

More often, we are in need of personal space. Sometimes we want to mix up with people and party but sometimes we need personal space to breathe in. This happens to everyone. You might have been through the phase when you start feeling uncomfortable because of the presence of a particular person. In technical terms, this is known as proxemics. Anthropologist Edward T. Hall explains four levels of proximity between two people. Let's discuss them one by one. (Cherry, 2019)

Intimate distance: Ranging between 6 and 18 inches, this indicates that two people are enjoying a closer relationship. They are comfortable with each other. Two people come at this distance while they are hugging or touching each other.

Personal distance: Ranging between 1.5 to 4 feet, this distance suggests that two people are family members or close friends. If two people keep this distance but are comfortable in their interactions, this suggests how intimate they are in their lives.

Social distance: Ranging between 4 and 12 feet, this physical distance exists between people who have acquaintance with each other. With a coworker, the distance will shorten while with a person whom you don't know well such as a plumber, you will keep it at 10 to 12 feet.

Pubic distance: Ranging between 12 to 25 feet, this physical distance is used in public areas when you are addressing a gathering or a class or giving a presentation to your staff. (Cherry, 2019)

Apart from that, if a person comes closer to you, this suggests that he is looking for a favor from you. On the contrary, if the other person moves away, this means there is a lack of mutual connection between you two. The above-mentioned distance is not something carved in stone. It differs in different cultures.

Mannerism

Winking is a normal act between friends and intimate people, but when a stranger wink at you, it appears invasive and offensive. Wink is generally a break in eye contact which suggests that the person is trying to disrupt the flow of conversation. On a lighter note, while cracking a joke, winking is absolutely fine. Winking without reason, tends to confuse the other person. So, steady eye contact is always the way to go.

If a person has placed his arms in an unnatural position, he is not sure of himself. He is not relaxed and is suffering from a lack of confidence. The conversation with an uncomfortable person tends to be unproductive and inconclusive.

Facial Interpretation

Reading one's facial expressions is an integral part of understanding his nonverbal behavior. We have already discussed some visible expressions like winking, blinking and many other expressions. In this section, I'll briefly discuss micro-expressions. They are brief and involuntary expressions that appear on a person's face. They have great importance because it is pretty hard to fake them. Let's discuss them one by one.

A person's eyebrows will appear to be raised with a slight curve. Their skin just below the brow will appear to be stretched. His forehead will have winkles and his eyelids will remain open for a while. His jaw will appear to be dropping and teeth will be slightly parted. Their mouth will remain normal with no signs of tension.

Pay close heed to a person's lips to detect the element of disgust in their disposition. Look out for if their upper lip appears to be raised or upper teeth appear to be exposed. Also, see if his nose has wrinkles and cheeks, raised. Any such sign shows that the person is feeling disgusted.

You can detect anger from micro facial expressions. She has slightly lowered her eyebrows or drawn them together. Other signs of anger are tension in the lower lid or bulging eyes. In addition to this, if their nostrils are dilated or their lower jaw seems to be jutting out, this also shows that they are in anger.

You also can detect happiness in other people by observing their faces. She is happy if her lips appear to be drawn back. Similarly, if her mouth is parted and teeth are exposed, this is an indication of happiness. Happy people have their cheeks raised eyelids lowered with wrinkles evident underneath. Another common sign is the appearance of crow's feet on the outside of the eyes. An important thing to note is that if she is not engaging her side-eye muscles to show her happiness, her happiness is fake.

Inner Instinct

Inner instinct or gut instinct guides the physical reactions that we give to the world around us. It is the feeling that we sense when our bodies are responding to the processing of information that is stored in our subconscious, as I have briefly explained earlier on. The main purpose of our gut instinct is to give us protection in the wake of unusual circumstances. Sometimes people cannot define it but they are relying on it to deal with worldly matters. Their gut instinct guides them through thick and thin. Its power and influence vary in different people depending on their experiences and spiritual state.

Some people call it a hunch while others label it as an inkling, but in general, it is dubbed as gut instinct or instant instinct. This is different from intuition as it is our primal wisdom, while intuition is our spiritual wisdom. Both humans and animals have gut instincts. In some cases, in animals, this feeling is more powerful than humans.

Take the example of a herd of zebras. Even when they cannot see the lions that are lurking behind the bushes, they somehow sense their presence. When one of them whinnies, the rest of the herd starts racing away for cover. If you are fond of Animal Kingdom documentaries, you might have seen such scenes. Similarly, big animals like elephants rely on their gut feeling to find food and water resources.

If you are a cat lover, you can see that your cat will change its mind once or twice before it jumps over from the second story to the first story. Have you ever heard any story of hikers who got lost in the mountain trails? They had to navigate through the mountains without any compass or anything else to take help from. One of them had a hunch to go to the east and the rest of them followed him. In the end, they had successfully reached the camp. Just imagine what would have happened, had that hiker ignored his hunch.

Sometimes you have a strong feeling that something has happened to your son who is at home. You ditch the office and drive back home to find him unconscious on the floor. If you take a closer look at the world around you and also at your own life, you will find that similar incidents have been happening to you.

Signs of Gut Feeling

There are certain signs to watch out for if you want to follow your gut. The top indication is a sudden feeling of fear, especially if it is uncalled for or totally out of context. The second is a powerful urge to accomplish something just like an inner pull. You might also suffer from chills and shivers in your body. Goosebumps on your arms and body in combination with tingles up your spine also indicate that there is something wrong.

One important thing to consider is that signs of gut feeling differ for different persons. For example, some people may not experience any of the above. Instead, they get nauseous or have physical uneasiness. A few people tend to get alarmed at times while only a handful of people hear instructions or warnings in a clear voice. You might have one sign or all of them.

Discuss Intuitive Cues

Intuition means "to look within." Some scientists term it as sophisticated intelligence. People are viewing it as something that helps us make decisions rather than being a magical thing that cannot be learned. Still, the fact remains that ancient and advanced civilizations like Buddhism, Hinduism and Islam have connected intuition to the human soul. You can see if your intuition is at work by following some simple signs. You will start feeling light and clear in your mind. No emotions will affect your judgment and you will be absolutely calm and relaxed, and even inspired. If you are observing similar signs in your body and brain, your intuition is most likely at work.

Aha Moment

Things come to a standstill at times. A person who is running a clothing factory complains that despite producing the best garments in the market, customers are drying up day by day. He had run a marathon marketing plan to boost up sales but to no avail. Is more marketing the only solution? Shifting the production model can be a viable solution to the problem. Brainstorming new ideas and selling techniques is what we usually do to solve this kind of situation. But what if ideas just stop coming to us? What if nothing seems to be working? Maybe he should freeze for a moment and do nothing. Yes, this works sometimes. He should just stop pursuing a solution to the problem. Instead, he should take a shower, start playing golf or maybe watch a movie. People hit upon amazing solutions to overdue problems when they detach them from the current scenario for a while.

The key to reach the aha moment is creating an environment that is full of silence as well as solitude. These conditions are essential for your brain to nurture these moments. Ultra-quiet places are always the best for making better decisions. Once you have found a quiet place for yourself, you have to start looking inward. Focus on the live stream of thoughts. You have to detach yourself from the outer world like your cell phone and any other thing around you. When the external information ceases to reach your brain, you will slowly start noticing the aha moment. Gradually, you will achieve the "idle" mode of your brain. It is important to know that you don't have to stress out your schedule to get the aha moment. Instead, find a few quiet moments on a daily basis to do this exercise. Also, try to turn off all the electronic gadgets at least for a few hours in a day so that you can leave your brain to wonder for a while.

Human Vibe

The vibe we give off is equally important for reading people as reading their body language. This is closely linked to intuition. We run away from some people and try to be close to some of them. More often, we hear people say that they feel good or bad vibe by being around some people. Some people really elevate our mood when we are around them, while others drain us out of our positive energy.

The impact of the human vibe can be felt when we are just inches or feet away from a person. Some cultures like the Chinese dub this invisible energy as life force, named as chi. Let's take a look at a few examples.

Sometimes, your spouse says sorry to you but you feel that he is not really sorry for his mistake. A coworker is trying to charm you but you know something is fishy out there. A classmate appears to be cheerful but you have already sensed the hidden anxiety. For example, we often say that depression is faceless. People wear a smile in front of others but in reality, they are broken. While most of them around a depressed college fellow ignore her condition, you are sure that she is not healthy at all.

You need to link a person's emotions with his energy to get to know them better. Reading people by human vibe is all about decoding their emotions. By reading people's energy, you can bring yourself in line with how you relate to them, and whether you feel comfortable with them or not. If you study this subject and master it, you are able to make some crucial decisions in an effective way. For example, you will never want to spend your life as a spouse with a person who will drain your energy. The same is the case with a coworker. Why should you consume your time sharing your meals with a coworker who leaves you feeble and unproductive after a single sitting? That's why it is important that you learn how to read the human vibe.

Presence

The first thing to learn while reading people's energy is sensing the presence of people. This is the overall effect that a person leaves on you when he or she is near you. You have to calculate it. A girl in your office may leave mysterious, joyful or sad effects on you. Try to make out if the person around you is pulling you toward her. When you are reading them from their presence, try to notice if the energy they give off is warm or cold. Is it like fresh air or stalled? Do you sense anger or depression when you are near them? Whether it is a friendly sense or an intimate one when she is near you. On the basis of these readings, you can decide how to shape the future course of your relationship with that particular person.

Eye Projection

Another important method to read the human vibe is to take a closer look at that person's eyes. Eyes are the ways to transfer positive and negative energy. In Islamic civilization, eyes are considered as the source to transfer spiritual energy. Sufi poets like Rumi greatly focused on the importance of a glance. They say that the brain transmits electromagnetic signals through eyes. Looking straight into the eyes of your pet releases oxytocin which builds up a trustful and peaceful relationship between you and your pet.

You should take your time when you are observing her eyes, then study what kind of feeling you have. Is it the feeling of love, care, calm or anger? Do her eyes look sexy? Do they intimidate you? People's eyes may feel hypnotic at times. Sometimes looking deeply in their eyes make you feel insecure. That's why you have to study the effects of cautiously. If you come across a negative person, try not to engage them or they will zone in on you. If you sense positivity, keep looking straight into their eyes. Feed on all the positive energy.

Physical Contact

We share our energies with people upon touching them by means of a handshake or a hug. Whenever you touch someone through a handshake, you will know whether the person makes you feel comfortable or not. Or do you just want to withdraw? Do their hands feel clammy? This is a sign of anxiety. They will make you feel anxious. If they hold your hands in a powerful grip that your fingers feel pained, this gives off aggressive energy.

Voice Tone

Last but not least is the tone of voice in which people speak to you. It will speak volumes about their emotions and feelings. The frequency of our sounds creates distinct vibrations. Does their tone soothe you and make you calm? If you observe that the voice tone of a person is so soft that you barely hear him, this shows signs of low self-esteem. If they are too loud, this shows anxiety or insensitivity. If they are fast-talkers in your first meeting, they might want to sell something to you.

Try to observe if people are laughing too much. If this is the case, they are lighthearted. But their laugh ought to be genuine. (Orloff, 2014).

Chapter 5

Lies – Why They Affect the Way You Analyze People?

L ies go undetected more often, so do liars. Lying is quite prevalent among youngsters and this behavior hardly does any harm at that age, but when you grow older and enter professional life, liars can be harmful to your professional and intimate life. Kids consider this habit as something fun to tease their school mates and friends from the neighborhood. When they don't get caught, they consider this behavior as a way to go in life. They integrate this behavior into their personality and use it later on for personal benefits. So, that's how lying as behavior makes its way in our characters.

If you don't nip the evil in the bud, the kids will see this as a baseline for building up a powerful lying pattern to be used in the future. When you are dealing with these grown-up kids, you feel at a disadvantage because they maneuver it so professionally that you realize it only when they have already achieved their goals. It is not that liars are impossible to detect. In fact, they are pretty easy to spot around us. All we need are a few techniques to make out if a person is telling you the truth or is concealing something from you. Before we move on to analyze the techniques, we need to analyze different types of liars to make the process of detecting liars easy and smooth.

Types of Liars

Let's discuss the difference between people who are quite professional at lying. There are certain signs and symptoms that you need to watch out to find out what type of liar you are dealing with. Let's see and analyze each category to gain more insight when you are analyzing people.

Pathological Liar

The first category is the pathological liars. Pathological liars are habitual and they tell a lie in response to any kind of stimuli. They are very good at lying because of the magnitude of practice that they do. They are pretty good at fabricating stories and it is very hard to detect when they are lying and when they are telling the truth. If only you can read their facial expressions and gestures, it is easy to detect them. Look out for the movement of their eyes. If they are trying to avoid direct eye contact, they are not telling you the right thing.

If you want to understand why people lie so casually, you have to understand the circumstances they went through. They adopt pathological lying as a defense mechanism. It is a way to make their way through severe circumstances without hurting themselves. These are not excuses to become a pathological liar but these are the driving factors that push a normal person to integrate this personality trait. By understanding the pushing factors, you will be able to understand why people lie in the first place. In this way, you can stop a pathological liar midway while is weaving his web.

Sociopath

These liars are considered as the worst types of liars. They lie to achieve personal benefits without caring about how it will affect the people around them. They have a heart made of stone and they don't care about other people's emotions and even their lives. In simple words, they feed on lying. Lying is their strategy to get worldly benefits at the cost of the feelings and lives of other people. They don't feel shame or guilt at all.

When you are confronted with these kinds of people, you need to walk cautiously by carefully reading the situation. The situation can go out of control any time and you will find yourself becoming their victim in a snap. The reason is that they can turn out to be amazingly manipulative when dealing with you. They are experts in lying and they are more often quite cunning.

When you are analyzing these kinds of people, you are likely to end up reaching a wrong conclusion because of misleading or insufficient evidence. If you are currently into a relationship with a sociopath liar, you should try to free yourself of the commitment. When you are convinced that the relationship is poisonous because of the lying habit of your partner, end the relationship. You can exhaust your option of changing that person before taking a decisive step. (5 Types of Liars and How to Recognize and Deal with Each, n.d)

By now, you might be thinking that liars are like parasites who drain you of emotions and energy. But we must not forget they too are humans. They are not monsters whose only treatment is to send them in exile out in the wild or kill them with the best weapon available. It is advised that if you detect the lying habit in someone close to you for the first time, you should approach them with kindness. Show them love, tact and affection according to the size and impact of the lie that they just weaved for you or any other person. Don't forget to furnish your evidence or the other person will get away with it by denying it altogether.

It is highly likely that some liars will defend their lies and continue with it when you try to confront them, but you should keep in mind that liars have mastered the art of manipulation. Keep yourself in full senses to get away with their manipulation. (5 Types of Liars and How to Recognize and Deal with Each, n.d)

White Liars

We often see white liars around us. White lies are not real lies. At least they are not as lethal as real lies are. In most cases, they are perfectly harmless, and you can say that white liars more often tell one or the other kind of truth, that's why people believe that they are not lying. Some weak hearted people use white lies in a bid to protect themselves from the truth if they are of the opinion that truth will be damaging or hurtful for them.

When you detect white lies, you should approach those people and try to rectify their ways. If you find out that the white lie has insignificant value, perhaps you ought to let it pass. Otherwise, you can ask the liar to mend his or her ways as it is not a good idea to base a relationship on lies no matter how harmless the lies are. If you fail to detect white lies or let them pass as fun, they may cause serious problems for your intimate relationships in the long run. (5 Types of Liars and How to Recognize and Deal with Each, n.d)

Compulsive Liars

Compulsive liars are habitual when it comes to lying, but unlike pathological liars, you can detect them and figure out how to deal with them quite easily. They are not expert enough to weave a net of truth around their lies to make them appear credible to people. They are easy to analyze because they don't wear a cloak of truth over their woven web of lies. When they speak, you can tell that they are lying because they display such kind of behavior. Things to note when you meet such a person are that they will start sweating, and also, they will never look into your eyes while telling a lie.

Compulsive liars can be further categorized into a habitual liar as well as a narcissistic liar. Habitual liars cannot refrain themselves from lying all the time. On the other hand, narcissistic liars make up stories about themselves. They tend to exaggerate things and like to embellish things about themselves. They will you stories how they confronted a dozen warriors and single-handedly defeated them. Other stories include how they turned out to be the hero of a number of situations like saving a girl from a raging fire. Most of the stories they tell may appear to be far-fetched. As per medical science, these kinds of people suffer from a narcissistic personality disorder. Lying becomes their habit because they feel deprived of their real lives. They have reached the conclusion that their real lives are boring and that no one is impressed with them.

How to Deal with Liars

There is a wide range of ways to deal with liars. This can be really difficult but the best approach is not to throw a fit of anger. The liar is likely to channelize your aggression toward diverting you from the subject. The best approach is to avoid getting carried away with their versions of events that you have concrete evidence of not being true. You can deal with liars by being polite and confronting them with the truth.

You have to understand the fact that all of us tell lies at one point or another. Sometimes we have to fabricate a lie to avert a crisis. Sometimes, you need to tell a lie because you don't want to hurt someone's feelings. These kinds of liars are easy to deal with because they tell a lie only to defuse a tense situation. White liars are also harmless unless they make it a habit to tell lies. What if you are confronted with a compulsive liar or a sociopath? They are habitual when it comes to telling lies.

Compulsive liars are not the easiest to deal with. In order to kill their sense of inferiority and inadequacy, they can go on to any extent to tell lies without caring for their effect on the lives of other people. They lack empathy and are unable to understand the extent of emotional turmoil that they bestow on the other people. Their dishonesty takes its toll on others. They are self-centered and can only think about their own benefit and profit.

These types of liars are the most difficult to deal with, but with greater understanding and practice, you can master the art. The first thing you should remember is to avoid confrontation with these kinds of people. They always try not to leave a trace of what they have done. When you confront them, they will come up with a new story to cover up their wrongdoing, in addition, they will become hostile in their attempt to invalidate your evidence. So, there is no point in confronting them. You have to make yourself believe that the person you are dealing with is not normal and he needs help. Think of him as a dysfunctional person who doesn't think normal. If you try to change them, they will resist any effort by hook or crook. So, you need to stop changing them. Just accept them as they are and deal with them as if they are normal. This will make them friendly toward you and it will be easier to deal with them.

The next step is to listen to what they say carefully. Don't trust it right away. It is better to retain the factor of doubt. Spare the room for verification of what they tell you. You should be careful about not letting them know what you are up to. When you are sure that the person is a compulsive liar, put a limit on the time that you spend with him; otherwise, they will keep draining you of energy and demoralize you.

These types of people don't merit your time and love. Avoid sharing your personal information and any other details with that person. Don't open up too much or they will use that information for their personal benefit. They can do that without thinking even once because of the fact that they don't have empathy for others. (Kloppers, n.d)

The next step you should take care of is that you must not expose a liar. You think that you have detected a liar and the liar also knows that. As per your impulse, you will rush toward your closest friends to tell them about that person in order to save them from his or her heinous behavior. Freeze and think for a moment. Is it really a good idea to tell others about him or her nature? The answer is a 'no.' In fact, it is pretty dangerous. The liar will behave like a suspect does on getting detected by cops. Move on in your lives as if nothing happened. Focus on what you are doing and you will be in complete comfort. In some cases, if the liar is bent on inflicting losses and pain on you, you have to do something about it. Even in these situations, think about the possible impacts of exposing them. Better have a comprehensive discussion on the subject with the people who are close to you.

When you have decided to expose a liar, you should do this carefully so that you don't paint him or her in a negative picture. Try to convince others that he or she did that out of sheer necessity. This will paint your picture positively in the eyes of the liar. That's how you can expose him and also succeed in gaining his sympathy. In fact, this can promote friendship between you two.

In severe circumstances in which the chances of confrontation are high and moving on also is not a good choice, the only way is to show that you understand why the liar committed that wrong act. Not only show them by gestures or expressions but also try to tell them in clear words that you understand why they did that. Tell that it is normal to do that for self-protection, and also tell them that you accept them. That's how we are actually telling them that what they did was wrong but we are forgiving them. This has the potential to change their hearts. Perhaps they decide to mend their ways.

The above method doesn't always work. Some people tell harmful lies without shame or regret. They even inflict serious losses on people by telling lies. They are the ones who ought to be exposed so that other people should be saved from their lethal actions. You must not fear of exposing them and getting into a direct confrontation. They have already inflicted losses on so many people that there will be hardly anyone left who will show sympathy toward them. The people whom he has done wrong will support you. When we are done exposing them, we should immediately part our ways with them and become more cautious.

Compulsive liars are without a doubt hard to deal with. There is no hard and fast rule for the purpose. You have to read the person and then tailor your reaction to suit the circumstances. Without much homework, you will only land in trouble.

Chapter 6

Adverse Effects of Misreading People

T his chapter is going to walk you through the effects of mixed signals. You will learn how people misread each other's signals and how it lands them in trouble or at least create a web of confusion among them. Reading people, though seems easy, is a tough nut to crack. If you miss out on a key signal and misinterpret it, you are going to misread someone's intentions. Bad intentions will be interpreted as good while good as bad. Similarly, wrong judgment will hamper our social connections or relationship with our colleagues.

This suggests that you should know the consequences of misreading people so that you may remain cautious. One wrong decision may land you in trouble. Mixed signals are dangerous in the sense that they confuse you, and confusion edges you off the right track. You should know what mixed signals are and how you can deal with them to avoid a crisis situation. This chapter also carries examples of mixed signals and the ways to tackle them wisely.

Mixed Signals

I have a friend named John who got a job at a grocery store. There he had a team of around a dozen people. As a good manager, he used to call a meeting every Thursday. Each meeting had an agenda that John followed in letter and spirit. John tells me that he wanted to be as handy to his staff as was possible. He used to help them in packing and putting groceries on the shelves for display.

John believed that he couldn't do more for the staff. Unlike most other bosses, John was a really good listener. He always welcomed criticism, suggestions and new ideas to improve the look of the store and boost sales. He was pretty satisfied with his role in the store. One day he welcomed criticism on his own performance in the store, so he requested his staff to criticize his shortcomings. Literally no one appeared at the meeting, suggesting that they had no issues with his style of running the store. After insisting for a week, one employee appeared in his office and opened up his heart. He said, "Mr. John, why do we think that we cannot do our jobs right. Why do you always come up to give us a hand? Don't you have confidence in our abilities?" This was completely shocking for John. He didn't think that his offer to help his staff would be perceived in another way.

John thought that by helping her staff, he would be able to identify with them. They will feel relaxed and satisfied, but the result was completely different from what he had thought. Instead of considering John a generous and kind person, his team felt a kind of inferiority complex.

This kind of scenario may happen and we don't even know about it. John's staff misunderstood his intentions. They perceived it as a lack of faith in their ability to do the job efficiently. These misunderstandings herald conflict as well as resentment, and this kind of misunderstanding is pretty common between couples. This story is also related to John. Compelled by his kind and affectionate nature, John wanted to hire a maid for her wife who was pregnant, and he did that accordingly. On the contrary, his wife thought that John didn't like the food she used to cook for the family just because he had passed critical comments on one or two dishes she had cooked. Despite the fact that you have explained that you are hiring the maid to relieve your wife of workload, but the seed of misunderstanding has already been sown.

Take a critical look at your own married life. There might be more than one occasion when you and your wife misunderstand each other for insignificant reasons. For example, you might be dining while your wife is telling a story to you. Although you are all ears to your wife yet she might find the act of your dining while she is speaking offensive. This may lead to a potential misunderstanding between you two. Similarly, you two have made a plan to go to a beach for sunbathing. Your wife feels sick and excuses herself from going with you. Although her excuse is genuine yet you might think that she doesn't want to go with you. Similar incidents of misunderstanding may happen when you two disagree on simple things like watching a movie together.

So, there is usually a big gap between what we say and how our listeners perceive it. The difference between real meanings and perceptions is not always a matter of egocentrism. Mixed signals are complex to understand but they have great importance when it comes to reading people. Mixed signals confuse you and land you in a blind spot where you cannot think clearly or see things how they are in reality. These signals cloud one's judgment of people and circumstances.

Take the example of a dating scene. You are dating someone who is not responding to your texts, but after some time, she reads your Whatsapp status or Facebook story. You will be confused. The point to understand is that we, as humans, lack perfection when it comes to expressing our thoughts. This is also true that we improve on our experiences and try to streamline our understanding of others' thoughts. Still, our true feelings tend to get hidden in how we translate them into actions and how we communicate through our speech. So, we can say that mixed signals are negative signals because that's how we are going to perceive them. One in hundred, if not thousands, will see something good in a mixed-signal.

So, should it go that way? Is it destined to be that way? There is an antidote to this problem. When you are confused about the inner feelings of a person, you should read their words coupled with their actions. But this demands practice, a lot of it, to decipher that hidden meaning accurately and perfectly.

Why Do People Give off Mixed Signals?

If you are receiving mixed signals, all burden is not upon you for reading her accurately. She also has to streamline lots of things. Mixed signals lead to miscommunication in most cases, and this affects the health of your relationship. Sometimes people intentionally use them to keep someone at arm's length because they just don't want to engage with them. For example, your fiancé is fed up with the relationship, but she cannot express it in words as it would be hard to hear and also, it would lead to an endless debate which she definitely wants to avoid. Here, she will start sending mixed signals to you. Like ignoring your texts but talking to you on phone or ignoring your call and responding to your texts, so that you take the hint that she doesn't want to be with you anymore. That's why first she will slow down the pace of the relationship and then she will say goodbye so that everything concludes making the least possible noise.

The story doesn't end here. Mixed signals don't always mean that the other person is trying to avoid you. It also is a way to cope with the stress that comes from getting intimated and close to other people. Your girlfriend might be going through this phase of stress, and you unknowingly end the relationship blaming her for intentionally avoiding you. Let's take a look at some mixed signals that sabotage relationships.

They Don't Meet up Your Expectations

There might come a moment in your life when you keep waiting on end for a special person in your life to respond to your texts or Whatsapp status. It is normal behavior to send and text and then expects a response to it right away. Absence of which can cause confusion and misunderstanding, and may mar your relationship in the long run. It is normal that the other person might be caught up in work. You will wait for the first few minutes but when a considerable length of time has passed, frustration will come to hit you hard. You will start feeling off about it.

It is possible that they will respond to you when they are free and when they find it convenient. In order to have a clear view of the circumstances, you should note if this kind of behavior has become a habit with them or not. One thing is clear from a recurrent behavior that the person is not fully dedicated to you.

Half-hearted Effort to Meet You

"I am dying to meet you. When will we meet? I am planning to drop in this weekend. Stay free." She texts you thrice a week but has not yet found time to come over on weekends and spend time with you. Every time she misses a weekend, she texts you saying that she remained busy. One or the other assignments keep her from coming over to you. She says that she has to juggle responsibilities and priorities. You remind her that she is placing other things as top priorities and ignoring you. People are not busy at all. It is all about priorities. When she has decided to meet you, she will find a way out. If she is not doing that, she has other things at top priorities. That's why she is unable to fulfill her commitment to you. Maybe she is sending you a mixed signal for a reason. Take the catch and make a decision.

She Doesn't Open up as She Should Be

When a relationship kicks off, you expect your partner to share everything with you like the names of her friends, information about her exes and lots of other things. It is this transparency that helps in cementing the foundation of your relationship. When the two of you have shared everything with each other, you will be able to form an emotional connection, which sets things off. Both you and your partner need to share their bit for a healthy connection. If you are sharing everything while she seems to be holding back, this is not a good omen for the relationship. The foundation will have cracks right from the start, which will eventually bring down the entire structure one day. Therefore, if you sense such a behavior, take it as a deliberately mixed signal. Analyze it and make a timely decision instead of delaying and regretting afterward.

Does Your Partner Flirt with Other People?

This turns out to be painful than other signals for lots of people, but this is also an important one to study if you want to make accurate assessments. This happens in thriller movies. The hero has a girlfriend who is a bit friendlier with his friends. At first, everything seems to be normal but slowly, you realize that she is up to something else. Do you remember a scene from any Hollywood movie in which hero plans for camping beside a lake along with his girlfriend and college fellows? At the campsite, she pays more attention to the friends of the hero. The hero gets confused at first due to the mixed signal. Then gradually, he realizes that something is fishy. His girlfriend is not actually interested in him. She is keeping all options open so that if one doesn't work out well, she could jump to the other.

The solution is not to frame allegations around her but keep patience. Ponder over how she is dealing with your friends. Note the dialogues, the gestures and the frequency of their meetings in addition to the time she spends with them. When you are sure that something is wrong, you should take her out for a walk at someplace where your friends couldn't reach to disturb you. Now you ask her in clear words about what is happening and why is it happening? You can request her to change her behavior because the current behavior unsettles you. If she truly cares for you, she will try to tone down her behavior and keep herself in check. If she doesn't try at all, take this mixed signal as a clear sign to make a decision. It is better to part ways than regret afterward.

She Cares for You When You Are Alone but Doesn't Show Affection When You Two Are in Public

Watch out for this mixed-signal carefully. She is ready to make out with you while you are at home. She is super comfortable while talking to you on end and watching a movie with you, but when you are out with friends for a hangout, she is unwilling to be seen with you. She just doesn't want to open up about her relationship with you. If your relationship is in its infancy, you should give your partner some time to adjust herself in your and her friend circles. When she is comfortable enough, the relationship will take a smooth road and move on well, but if she continues to behave like that after a while, you should take this signal with caution. Perhaps she made a hasty decision and now she is regretting. She may be pointing toward the underlying tension that exists in your relationship. Maybe she doesn't want to be seen with you anymore in public but is too polite to tell you so.

Remember that when a person truly loves you, their words and actions go on well. If she promises you to show up at your office when your boss throws a party for you and she doesn't keep it, these signals should be taken as serious. Like all other mixed signals, you have to give her some time. After three to four incidents, you will be better positioned to make a decision.

Chapter 7
Analyzing Verbal Cues

In order to know the difference between the truth and deception, you have to follow certain cues. The signs of lying are not clear; hence they are hard to understand. In addition, you cannot always be sure whether a person is lying or not. By practice, you can be able to tell if someone is lying to you or not easily. The rule is simple. When we are lying, we are deviating from how we behave naturally. We have to make an effort to look truthful while we are lying; that's why if you know how a person behaves naturally, you can easily tell when they are lying by tracing the difference in their behavior. The difference can be the inclusion of certain words or phrases that he normally doesn't use.

Look for Deviations in Their Words

Inconsistencies can help you distinguish the truth from the lie. For example, a person at your office tries to convince you that he didn't meddle in your documents. If he is telling the truth, he will not care what you like to listen to from him. Otherwise, he will formulate a plan in his brain. He will brainstorm what words and phrases should be used so that he may look truthful before you. The phrases like, "I didn't do that. I wasn't in the office at that time. How could if do it?" should be enough to put him under suspicion. In addition, he will repeat these words and phrases again and again. Experts believe that this kind of repetition buys them more time to think and fabricate another phrase that could convince you that he didn't do it.

Another verbal cue is that he will tell you more than you need to listen. Chances are high that he is telling you a lie. Liars talk too much because they have made it a habit to fabricate lies. They're uncalled for openness should be enough to alarm you.

Another indication of a liar is that they find it pretty hard to speak when you try to ask questions from them. They will stammer, lose words and find them entirely speechless. The reason for this kind of behavior is psychological. Their mind is not ready for rapid questions. Liars make up stories when you ask them a question. After one or two questions, they find them at a loss. Another reason is that our automatic nervous system malfunctions during stressful times. This dries them out of answers, which is an indication that they are telling lies. Also, watch out if they are biting or pursing their lips or not. Any such behavior is an indication of a liar.

Learn to Ask Right Questions

Parents have to believe what their kids say to them. When they say they were with their best friends whom you know very well, you believe them without investigating the truth. But when they tell the same thing again and again, this means there is something fishy in the bottom of the story. Teenagers want to do lots of things that pass their mind and to make it possible, they tend to tell lies to their parents so that you their parents or teachers approve of their activities. When they suspect that a particular activity would not be approved, they tell outright lies. This is the time to worry.

If you level allegation of lying against them, they will become hostile to you right away, and this will only make them more stubborn. That's why you need to be tactful to make them realize that their lie is not working without them knowing that you are manipulating them. That's where you need to use the technique of Volatile Conundrum. Try to create a scene. Ask your son the right question. Ask him where he went with Jimmy, the name he used to deceive you. Jimmy is his classmate whom you approve of if your son remains with him.

"You got home pretty late at night."

"Where did you go with Jimmy?"

He would say that they were at McDonald's to celebrate the birthday of their friend from school.

Here you have to come up with your own version of the story. "Really? I heard that a minute fire broke out at McDonald's due to short-circuiting. Did everything go well? When did the fire brigade reach the site?"

Now, this is the momentum where your son will be caught in a conflict. Whether to approve your version of the story or deny it altogether? If he approves of it right away in a snap decision, you have successfully caught a liar without confronting him. If he disputes the fact that the fire didn't break out but in reality it did, again you have successfully caught a liar. In this way, you have successfully put your kid in a Volatile Conundrum situation.

Knowing How and When to Read Verbal Cues

All of us use verbal cues almost every day. Have you ever wondered how do you communicate with people? What are the ways in which you communicate with them? Communication is not a simple process that you can easily understand. It is rather a complicated process that is so detailed that you cannot miss out on a single nuance without miscommunicating what you have on your brain. There are little things that you take into account during communication such as your reaction when someone tells you a joke. Whether you should laugh, smile, or don't do anything at all. We usually get ready to laugh when we are sure that the person has delivered her punch line of the joke. Some laughs are spontaneous. You just cannot wait to understand before you laugh whether it is the punch line on which you are laughing or not. So, that's complicated. What if you laugh before the punch line, would it not sound awkward? What if you have delayed the laugh? Now the other person will be in an awkward situation.

You have to look for verbal cues when you are communicating with someone. In communication, cues are generally considered as prompts that you can use to show others that it is time for them to issue a response or give a reaction. A verbal cue can be a word, a pause in language, rise in the tone or fall in it, or anything else related to speech. For example, I asked my friend, "Shall we try our luck in starting a new business for the two of us?" Now I have put up a question for my friend and I expect a response from him. There should be an answer or the communication will hit a stumbling block.

Verbal cues are more important when we have to teach children at home or at school. Children are not so accustomed to understanding non-verbal gestures like facial expressions and body language. You have to explain everything in words before them. When a teacher has taught kids a lesson on the whiteboard. She asks them, "Can anyone draw a circle on her page like the one that is drawn on the whiteboard?" She will for sure use nonverbal gestures like pointing her hands toward the circle and toward the pages that are put in front of them on the desks. So, that's how with the help of clear words teachers are able to communicate their questions and instructions to the students.

Take another example. The teacher has taught the kids about circles and the way to draw them. They come the next day to the class. The teacher plans to take a surprise test about circles. She will draft a question in her head that will be easier for the kids to grasp and respond to. Perhaps she says to them, "You remember what we learned yesterday?" At least a few of them will respond in the affirmation. Now she says, "Who will come up and draw a circle on the whiteboard?" This is the question that the kids will understand and respond to you accordingly.

Direct and Indirect Verbal Cues

You need to know the words when communicating with other people. Direct verbal cues are clear statements or instructions. Parents are quite skillful in these verbal cues because they have to raise kids. Even new parents find out ways to train the children because verbal cues are integrated into our nature. Let's see some example of verbal cues that a child understands easily and integrate into his or her brain to use it in the future.

- Come to me.

- Go and clean your bedroom.

- What are you chewing?

- What are you studying?

- Why have you come so late from school?

- What are you thinking about?

- Have you brushed your teeth?

- Did you put the blender on the rack?

- Where are your books?

- How did your exam go last week?

So, these are the questions that we ask our kids every day. These examples contain clear instructions for the kids that's why they understand them right away and respond accordingly.

The second type of cues is indirect verbal cues. These also are considered as prompts but they are quite less obvious than the direct cues. I mean they are just not direct questions with a clear question mark at the end. When a teacher shows up in the class and puts the following questions?

- Has anyone seen my pen?

- Has anyone got an electric clock?

- Have you understood the concept well?

- Does anyone know how to draw a circle?

• Will anyone show up at the desk to draw a circle?

These questions are not specific to a single student. Instead, these are general questions. Only the students who will relate to them will respond to them accordingly. In simple words, we can say that indirect verbal cues throw the ball in the court of the listener. It is him or her who will decide whether to respond or not, how to respond and when to respond. The prompt in indirect verbal cues are not directed to any specific person. See the following examples:

• What are you going to eat today?

• What have you done from dusk till dawn today?

• What work have you done to clean the house?

• How did you bake the cake?

• How are you going to get a job in NYC?

• What are you going to do in the evening?

Chapter 8

Looking into One's Own Self

I t is a proven fact that magic crystals, tarot cards, palmistry and astrology can help develop your psychic skills but still, the most direct and effective method to know about yourself is to connect with your own mind. If you really want to connect with your own self, you will have to invest considerable time in reading your habits and how you behave. Just like meditation, you have to stay away from television, radio, and mobile any other activity that would engage you to mind. There should be no children or pets around you while you are on your way to finding yourself. You can turn on light music if it helps collect your thoughts but you can also sit in complete silence if it makes you comfortable. Let's take a look at some key benefits of self-knowledge.

Benefits of Self-Knowledge

There are certain benefits that you need to take a look at in order to be motivated for exploring yourself.

• Knowing yourself will offer you a special kind of pleasure and happiness. You are in a position to tell other people who are. Your expression is confident and smooth. When you know what you desire for, you can express it in simple words.

• Knowing yourself helps you improve your decision-making. When you tend to know yourself, you are better able to make certain choices about the world. These can span from making small decisions to big ones like choosing your partner. You are more ready to tackle the problems of your life and also find solutions for them.

• Knowing yourself offers you self-control. The ability to know yourself helps you understand what motivates you to put a stopper to bad habits and what is needed to adopt good habits.

• Good knowledge of your own self helps you resist social pressures that are constantly mounting upon you from one or the other sides. When you know what you like and dislike, you are more ready to say yes and no to certain people and their proposals.

• This also makes you more willing to tolerate and understand other people. You are in a good position to know your own struggles which helps you identify with other people. This instills more tolerance in your personality. (Selig, 2016)

Let's see how you can know yourself.

Concentrate on Yourself

Before you go on to knowing yourself, you should clear your mind first of any intrusive or lingering thoughts that come to obstruct your mind. Bring yourself in a position in which you are the least distracted. Just focus on the current moment. You can try to focus on an imaginary point in your brain. Stabilize that point and try to find a grounding place where you find harmony. You need to focus on that point until your brain is free of negative thoughts. Concentrate on the white light of your consciousness. Feel the calm this state has brought to you. When you are no more distracted by negative thoughts, you can move on to the next step.

Ask Questions

Throw questions before your psychic self. This is where you can start thinking about your life and get answers from your own self. Before going into this procedure, you need to have a clear idea of what you have been trying to find out about you. It is always a better idea to jot down these questions on a piece of paper and memorize them. Now ask them from yourself. See the following examples:

- What is the perfect job for you?

- Where do you want to live?

- What type of partner do you want to have for you?

Try to be as clear as possible in asking questions. Vague questions will only produce muddled answers.

If you are doing it for the first time, it will be hard to get answers in the first go, so if your brain is empty of answers, don't take it to heart. Instead, keep trying to explore yourself. Give yourself time and space to settle on what you are trying to ask it. Keep your body and emotions in a fair check. You might feel unexplained sensations in your body or some emotional reaction. Don't ignore them. Note them down and try to see what they are trying to explain.

Gradually, you will be able to find the much-needed answers to your questions. Persistence and the right practice are keys to it. If you start curbing your emotions, you are binding your brain which is not good. Let every emotion and feeling flow naturally so that they may aid you in finding the right answers.

Know Your Personality

You should have complete knowledge of your personality. You think that you know yourself because you know who you want to meet, what you like in food and what you dislike, how you want your partner to be and behave. But have you ever experienced a situation in which you couldn't explain how you reacted in a certain way? We deal with certain people and things which we regret later on and even feel ashamed of. Still, we cannot explain why we reacted that way. How do you react to failure, success, a challenge or a bad day? All these things matter much.

Find out Your Core Values

Your core values, moral codes, and principles always remain dear and near to your heart. There are certain values on which you just cannot compromise. These values will ultimately affect your decision-making ability, the power to resolve conflicts, your way of communication and your day-to-day living style. Find out what they are by deep introspection, as I stated in details at the start of the chapter. Are they honesty, flexibility, integrity or security?

Are you soft-hearted, dedicated to the cause of others, prone to learning, wise or a leader? Once you have agreed on what your core values, you be more than ready to analyze other people and also mend your own ways when you stray away from the right path. (be your own psychic – 5 steps to give yourself a psychic reading, n.d)

Know Your Body

Our body is as complex as our brain is. Whenever you start to know it, it changes. When we are children, it is pretty different than when we get old. It remains a piece of a mystery until death because we don't take an interest in exploring its limits. It is full of surprises. Sometimes these surprises are positive while at other times, they are absolutely shocking. Did you ever think what your breathing pattern is? What are your abilities? How flexible are you? How much balance can you bring in your walking pattern? (be your own psychic – 5 steps to give yourself a psychic reading, n.d)

There are times when we say no because our body has reached a certain limit. I cannot do this or I cannot do that. Our body feels challenged. Here you need to take the time to become intimate with your own body such as your strengths and weaknesses. Whether you are comfortable in cold weather or hot weather or balmy weather are things that you must know about you. Many people claim that they know themselves but in reality, they are missing out on clarity. They are just not clear about their mind and vision. (be your own psychic – 5 steps to give yourself a psychic reading, n.d).

You Need to Know Your Dreams

All of us have dreams of a great work future, kids and a luxurious lifestyle. We dream about so many things that we get confused which is the thing that we want more. What are our preferences? Knowing dreams are important and they are worth going after. Get to know them and prioritize them in your brain so that when someone asks you, you are able to speak about them clearly without stammering or repeating.

If you are confused about a dream, ask yourself if you want to do a certain thing. For example, you want to become an interior designer. Gather all the details about this profession. Now ask yourself if you can accept this profession with all its intricacies and liabilities. If you find the answer in affirmative, you need to integrate your dream in your daily pursuit of goals. If you find out that the dream existed in your mind without any reason and that you are not sure whether to pursue it or not, just discard it and never let it distract you in the future. (be your own psychic – 5 steps to give yourself a psychic reading, n.d).

Know What You Like

We believe that we know what we like but in reality, this is not true. When someone knows himself, he is highly confident when dealing with others and doing some kind of work. The confidence is evident in his acts and speech. Almost every one of us gets carried away with the popularity of things thinking that we like them but the feeling wears away with time, leaving you confused.

Knowing yourself means that you know your likes and dis-likes up to the extent that you are able to write them down on a piece of paper without thinking much when you are asked to do that. Ask yourself the following questions. (be your own psychic – 5 steps to give yourself a psychic reading, n.d).

• What are the foods that you like the most?

• Who are the people you like to meet more often or who give you a pleasurable feeling?

• Which fruits do you love to eat?

• Which vegetables are your favorite?

• Which family members make you feel comfortable when they come to meet you?

• Which friends are annoying to meet?

• Do you like mobile games?

• What type of clothes do you want to wear?

You need to start learning by looking into the mirror. Sort out what you like and what you don't. Now all you have to do is to stay true to your likes or dislikes. If you keep doing what you don't like and also ignore what brings you joy, you are doing great injustice to yourself. In fact, you have become ready to give up your own personality. In simple words, you are not going to be happy. On the other, hand, if you take care of your likes and dis-likes, you are more likely to be happy. (be your own psychic – 5 steps to give yourself a psychic reading, n.d).

Practice makes you perfect. The more you practice, the better you will get on reading people. When you know yourself, you are better able to see others in a clear.

References

Be your own psychic – 5 steps to give yourself a psychic reading. (n.d). Retrieved from https://www.micheleknight.com/articles/psychic/psychic-ability/be-your-own-psychic-5-steps-to-give-yourself-a-psychic-reading/

Cherry, K. (2019). Understanding Body Language and Facial Expressions. Retrieved from https://www.verywellmind.com/understand-body-language-and-facial-expressions-4147228

Chu, M. (2017). The Truth About How Gut Instincts Really Work. Retrieved from https://medium.com/the-mission/the-truth-about-how-gut-instincts-really-work-d665425f1eb1

English, J. (2019). 5 Basic Body Language Signals of Manipulators. Retrieved from https://drwebercoaching.com/5-basic-body-language-signals-of-manipulators/

How To Read People Like the FBI. (2018). Retrieved from https://www.thrivetalk.com/how-to-read-people/

Kloppers. M (n.d). Dealing with Liars. Retrieved from https://www.mentalhelp.net/blogs/dealing-with-liars/

Orloff, J. (2014). The Power of Surrender: Let Go and Energize Your Relationships, Success, and Well-Being [pdf]. Retrieved from https://www.amazon.com/

Power-Surrender-Energize-Relationships-Well-Being/
dp/0307338215/ref=as_li_ss_tl?ie=UTF8&redirect=true&link-
Code=sl1&tag=theminwor01-20&linkId=7bec015a8cfbec80e5b-
b69f63a7ca784

Scott, R. (n.d). How to Read Body Language – Revealing
the Secrets Behind Common Nonverbal Cues. Retrieved from
https://fremont.edu/how-to-read-body-language-revealing-the-
secrets-behind-common-nonverbal-cues/

Selig, M. (2016). Know Yourself? 6 Specific Ways to Know
Who You Are. Retrieved from https://www.psychologytoday.
com/us/blog/changepower/201603/know-yourself-6-specific-
ways-know-who-you-are

9 Personality Types – Enneagram Numbers. (n.d). Retrieved   from   https://www.theworldcounts.com/life/poten-
tials/9-personality-types-enneagram-numbers

$$\boxed{\text{Part} - \text{II}}$$

HOW TO TALK TO STRANGERS

How to Master the Art of Talking to Strangers, Truly Connect with People and Make a Killer First Impression

Chapter 1

Getting Over Your Fear of Small Talk

"Small talk is the biggest talk we do."

- Susan Roane

I n today's world there are many opportunities to interact with others. Work, meetings, volunteer events, schools, community events, social gatherings, parties and the list goes on and on. We've all been somewhere and have borne witness to those individuals who seem to effortlessly and beautifully maneuver the crowd, sparking conversation with everyone in their path.

Then there are others of us that stop cold in our tracks. The idea of walking into a room, not knowing anyone (or maybe even a few people) and faced with the idea of interacting or making small talk, freezes us in our tracks. This is where it becomes a problem, when the fear of saying things in casual conversation takes over. Facing this anxiety can make going out, having a date, attending a party or socializing at all, mildly stressful to miserably intolerable.

The way we approach life can be determined by our mindset. Instead of being a little quirk in our personality, our mindset shapes our perception and shows us what's possible. A inflexible, unyielding mindset causes us to avoid failure, at any cost. But a flexible, accepting mindset turns mistakes and challenges into learning opportunities.

What is a Growth-mindset?

When someone believes their capabilities are developed through strategy, hard work and feedback from others, they have a growth mindset. These people usually accomplish more than people with a fixed mindset (those people that think their talents are God-given gifts). Usually this is because they put more energy into learning and less worrying about looking a certain way.

A growth mindset isn't always easy to maintain. We all have our individual fixed-mindset triggers and they tend to show up when we face challenges, when someone confronts or criticizes us or we compare ourselves to others. Then we fall into the old traps of insecurity, defensiveness and other not-so-awesome responses that don't exactly foster our growth.

While it can be challenging to embrace a growth mindset it can be so instrumental in our change. When we put growth mindset into practice, we come to a better understanding of who we are, what we stand for and how we want to navigate the future. Growth mindset also helps us remain optimistic and confident in the face of challenges.

Changing your limiting beliefs

What are our beliefs? They are simply habituated perceptions that have been built overtime. They can conjure old memories, pleasure or pain and our memories are based on how we interpret and mentally visualize our experiences.

Beliefs are assumptions we make about ourselves, about others, and about our expectations of the world. Based on our previous experiences we all have ideas and opinions on how things should work. We not only make these assumptions about our own life but we infer it for other people too. We use our beliefs as moors, helping us express our understanding of our world and what's going on in it.

How to Stop Being So Self-Conscious

Being self-conscious is a tough one and one we all face from time to time. When you're self-conscious it can feel like you're on stage and everyone in the audience is watching you intensely. I think logically you know that isn't true but it's sure how you feel.

Do you remember the last time you felt that awkward? Kinda cringe-worthy, right? You probably fidgeted a lot, maybe pulled on your sleeves and folded and unfolded your arms. When you feel like the whole room is looking at you, it's hard to stop feeling self-conscious.

While it can make you feel inadequate it doesn't always have to be that way. It's really just a state of mind. That might be a hard one for you to understand but that's all it really is. You think you don't measure up but again, how much truth is in that?

Here are a few ways to help you control those paranoid and controlling thoughts:

1. Shrug Away Pesky Thoughts

I know... easier said than done. But to eliminate self-con-
sciousness you're going to have to practice just shrugging it away.
Don't agree with them, just swipe them away. Now I didn't say
"pretend they don't exist". They exist not just for you but for
everyone walking the planet. You have to acknowledge they're
there but you don't have to agree with them.

2. Don't Put People on a Pedestal

Here's a situation a lot of people have been in. You're at
work and been asked to lead a meeting. Ugh. Dread sets in and
that's because you think everyone else knows more than you. You
feel inadequate. While there may be people in a room that know
more than you, you have to stop putting them on a pedestal. They
are no better than you are.

Remember, they are human just like you. They have moments they're embarrassed and self-conscious themselves. They
don't always have it all together and most times probably feel the
same way you do. So, stop pretending they are somehow better
than you.

3. Imagine Your Best Friend in This Same Situation

What if your best friend came to you and told you about the
date they walked into and felt immediately inadequate. Or the
time they went to that networking event and hung out in the cor-
ner all night, too intimidated to mingle. What advice would you

give them? Probable a pep talk reminding them how awesome they are.

So, the next time you're feeling shifty in a situation, imagine the advice you'd give your friend. Now give it to yourself. You deserve the same pep-talk and love session your friend does.

4. Accept Yourself ("Faults and All")

We all have faults. Something in us that makes us feel awkward and less-than-special. All you have to do is accept those faults and recognize every single person walking this planet comes equipped with their own set of faults too.

And focus on what you can do and what you are good at. That way when you walk into a party or crowd and you start to feel fidgety, remember your value and significance, regardless of your (perceived) imperfections.

5. Seriously Though, No One's Paying Attention

This is one I came to realize the older I got. I'm still reminding myself of this all the time but people truly aren't paying attention to you. They are so jumbled up in their own thoughts, struggles and worries with their internal spotlight shining bright on their own insecurities, they aren't looking at you. They aren't memorizing your every move and your every word and secretly criticizing you in their head. They're too busy wondering if they have something in their teeth to think about you.

So yes, while someone might notice your cheeks initially turn red or you pronounced a word incorrectly, no on lingers there. They aren't remembering it past the moment. Don't exaggerate it in your own head. They might have seen it happen but soon enough they're back in their own thoughts.

Small Talk Isn't Silly. It Serves a Purpose

Sometimes small talk gets a bad rap; a lot of backlash. People complain that small talk is beneath them and they're simply too important to discuss the weather. Yes, sometimes it does feel boring or shallow but it certainly serves a purpose. That's why it's important to learn.

Small talk leads to bigger talk. The conversation can go deeper and you can make a connection through small talk. It's the gateway towards forbidden topics. Sounds juicy but I simply mean it can take you from the benign... to the really heart-felt connections.

See with small talk you're giving people an opportunity to see if they are comfortable with you and asking themselves if they want to go deeper. You start talking about the weather which leads to hot weather destinations which leads to travel talk and who you've met along the way and suddenly you're learning something real about the other person. Something you wouldn't have without small talk.

Here is a breakdown of the reasons behind the importance of small talk:

1. Small Talk Builds up Trust

Some would argue the topic of small talk (that's to say the actual topic you're discussing) is immaterial. It's the gesture of time. It's the idea you've just spent your time and energy exchanging stories and ideas and it's establishing that a connection is taking place. Nothing else would be possible without this period of trust-building. Most people don't just dive into deep conversation without creating boundaries and parameters. These set the foundation for free and easy rapport that may at first appear to be of little consequence, until you see how it was the stepping stone towards a deeper trust.

2. Small Talk Lays the Foundation for Making Special Requests

We rarely start a conversation from ground zero. We rarely start a conversation until the other person volunteers some information that sounds like a good place to start. This can't happen without small talk. Seems pretty obvious but until you "break the ice" you won't have any idea where to even start a conversation. So small talk away.

3. Small Talk Can Uncover Important Information

When you first meet someone, you have no idea of their status, their importance or who they are in any particular circles. No one is going to walk up to you and say "Hi, I'm the President of XYZ Company and we're hiring. You look like a good fit. Call me Monday morning." Or "Hi there. I get this distinctive feeling we'd hit it off. Want to have dinner Saturday night?"

Directness in small talk sometimes pushes us toward awkwardness and uneasiness and it has the power to scare you off no matter how beneficial the conversation appears to you. Thatt's start with small talk to build up a momentum in conversation.

4. Small Talk Has the Power to Break the Deadlock in Conversation

Chatting or introducing yourself to people in your everyday life might seems unimportant or offhanded but it might come in handy down the road. Say you're locked out of your apartment or your office. If you've engaged in small talk with your security guard or maintenance person, they're going to be more likely to help you out.

You build rapport and trust with those people and that trust can help you out in certain situations. Small talk may appear to be small but it has the power to create a powerful bond between two people.

5. Small Talk Brings Forth Affection Among People

Has it ever happened to you that you plan a hang out with a someone near you? Even on the phone. It may feel like it takes you nowhere but it will signal to that person that you care. You can go for an intense session of conversation and go really deep with this person at times but keeping things light still engages the other person and tells them "I like hanging out with you."

Practice Makes Perfect - Just Do It Already

Small talk has a bad reputation for being frivolous—so much so that some people avoid it at all costs. But if you can make small talk meaningful and genuine (read: even about the weather) it can be the starting point for a new relationship, and even a meaningful career contact.

The best way to do it? Just do it already. It sounds scary and overwhelming and the very thought of it might make you fidget and break out in a small sweat, but I promise you it only gets easier. Make a point of sharing small talk with 3 people a day. You initiate it. You put yourself out there and make the first step. I promise within a few weeks it will start to feel like second nature and the scary will be replaced with excitement. Give it a try.

The most effective way to overcome your anxiousness when meeting someone new, is to make a killer first impression. In the next chapter we'll talk about how to make a great first and lasting impression. Read on...

———————

Takeaway:

- Change your limiting beliefs and watch how things change for you.

- Overcoming your self-conscious beliefs will open up a world of new discovery.

- Small talk isn't silly. It plays a really important role in life.

- The more your practice the art of small talk, the better you'll become.

Top 10 Mistakes That Destroy Your Charisma... and How to Avoid Them.

Mistake 1: Not Actively Introducing Yourself

You should enter a group or circle and instantly make eye contact, offer a handshake and then just be yourself. If someone is in a conversation, politely wait until there's a lull and then say something like "Sorry to interject, I just wanted to introduce myself."

Mistake 2: Failing to Introduce Your Friends in Social Interactions

If you're bringing along a friend or date to a social situation, make sure you introduce them to the other people you'll be mingling with. This shows respect and makes things a lot less awkward. How you treat the people in your life is a direct reflection of you. So, make it a good one.

Mistake 3: Talking Forever About Things Nobody Cares About

Just because you can talk Gibson versus Fender guitars for hours on end...not everyone else can. Or more importantly, wants to. It's great to bring up interests and ideas - it's how conversations start. But the more detailed you get, the more likely the other person is bored. Don't irritate people by re-telling last night's weird dream in detail. Trust me, no one cares. Don't waste other's time. It doesn't reflect well on you.

Mistake 4: Not Soliciting Feedback in Conversation

Sort of along the lines as above, not soliciting feedback feels like a one-sided conversation. Just check-in and see if people are responding to your story. If you don't hear an occasional 'wow' or 'you're kidding', pay mind and know it's time to wrap up your story. If you pause and they don't ask a probing question, they don't want to know. Not looking for feedback isn't winning you any favors.

Mistake 5: Being Judgmental of Others

When you're sharing yourself with other people, you want your truth and true personality to show through. Just remember not everyone is going to agree with you but you're courageous just for finding your voice.

Give the same courtesy to others. No matter who they are, what occupation they have and any other attributes that might make you draw conclusions. They have the courage to share themselves and nothing kills charisma more than prejudice.

Mistake 6: Trailing off or Mumbling

I've got to say I've been guilty of this. Usually when the setting is loud and I feel like my story isn't landing... I'll trail off. I catch myself and laugh inwardly thinking how silly I must look. I've come to realize you have to keep others engaged and speak with confidence and assuredness. Your cool factor diminishes the moment you mumble.

Mistake 7: Replying to Questions with One Word or Too Simple Answers

When someone asks you a question, have the courtesy to answer them in full. Don't give one-word answers. If they're asking you something they are want to engage in conversation. Find a way to expand and offer them something more than a yes or no. This is an opportunity to share yourself and make a connection. Charismatic people know how to keep conversation flowing.

Mistake 8: Constantly Whining/Complaining

Do you like listening to someone else complain about their stuff? Talking about a frustration is one thing. After all no one's life is perfect. But lamenting and expanding on our misery is plain boring and honestly puts you in a bad light. No one likes a complainer. Keep your whining to a minimum.

Mistake 9: Not Remembering Names

This is a trick suggested by master influencer Dale Carnegie. He says when you're introduced to someone you should repeat their name back to them. "Nice to meet you Lizzie." If you still didn't catch their name ask them to spell it for you. Remembering names and using them in conversation gives off an air of confidence and charisma.

Mistake 10: Lacking Principles or Conviction or Ideas

In other words, be yourself. We all enter into situation with our set of insecurities along with this weird societal pressure to fit in somehow. As a result, we aren't our authentic selves in conversation. We pretend to be something other than who we really are and then we don't know where we stand on issues. We come off as flaky.

Just be yourself and stick with what you truly believe. There are no rights or wrongs -only who you are. People might disagree with your position but that doesn't mean you're wrong. When you have strong convictions and principles you appear confident and people will respect a person that stands out rather than conforms.

Chapter 2

Seven Seconds to Make a Killer First Impression

"People sometimes talk about the power of first impressions, and believe me, there is truth to it."

- Ann Brashares

Importance of Making a Good First Impression

We all know the saying it takes one chance to make a great first impression. How about one glance? They say it takes only 7 seconds for someone to see you, evaluate you and set up an opinion. 7 seconds! In that short of time they form an opinion on the basis of how you behave with people, your gestures, your mannerism and the way you dress up for formal and informal occasions.

So, every time you encounter someone new; every time you head to a meeting or are introduced to someone at a dinner party... an impression of you is formed. And a lot of times that first impression sets the tone for what comes next.

That being said, here are a few things to consider the first time you meet someone new:

1. Be on time

Now I'm not always great at this one. And the irony is I actually really dislike being late. But somehow, I always am. Mind you only a few moments but still when meeting someone for the first time, I make an honest effort.

When you're meeting someone new for the first time they aren't interested in "why you're late". They don't care. All they know is you were late and from that point forward you'll be labelled with the late title. So, plan to arrive early. Even if you need to circle the block or sit in your car. Allow for flexibility for things like weather, traffic issues, getting lost. Arrive early. Not late. It creates a good first impression.

2. Appropriately Present Yourself

When you present yourself to someone for the first time, they have no precedent. They don't know who you are and how you exist in the world. So, your appearance is typically the first clue they have. They make assumptions based on how you present yourself.

Not don't worry. You don't have to have cheekbones of a super model and the closet of Madonna. The key to a great first impression is just to be yourself and present the best version of that. You know the saying "a picture is worth a thousand words". Well the picture is you! You need to show them who you are.

Keep mind the way you dress. Think about where you're going and who you're meeting then determine what's appropriate or not. What you wear will vary based on whether you're meeting in an office high-rise or cocktails at the trendy new restaurant. If you're meeting with a super creative individual, you might not want to wear a pinstripe suit. That said as long as you're comfortable and feeling confident, be you. Just be aware of the context.

3. Be Yourself

Like I just said above, be you. So, making a first impression sometimes means "fitting in" a little bit. If you're nervous about the meeting, you might have to conform at first to make a good impression. BUT that doesn't mean you lose yourself by pretending to be something you are not.

If you want to capture their attention and make a good impression, be your authentic self. In doing so you'll feel more confident, it will go towards building trust and earning the respect from people you meet along the way.

4. A Confident Smile Matters

As the saying goes, "Smile and the world smiles with you." When you smile it automatically puts the other person at ease. It suggests warmth and kindness. To create a good first impression, show those pearly whites.

5. Being Open and Confident Is the Best Body Language

I think we all know body language can often speak louder than words.

Use your body language to show your confidence and self-assuredness. Even if you aren't feeling it, by projecting it you fool others and a lot of times, yourself. Stand tall, smile, put your shoulders back, make eye contact, say hello. All of this helps you show confidence and it puts the other person at ease, allowing for comfort and conversation.

6. Use Small Talk

Throughout this book we talk about small talk and how important it is. When you first meet someone, conversations are based on a verbal give-and-take. So have a small list of questions you might want to ask. Or listen and learn something about the person. Do they like running? Do they have other hobbies? Any local charity they are interested in? What do you have in common? These are great ways to start and keep a conversation flowing.

Dress the Message

I know we already covered this but we're dedicated another little section to this.

See, like it or not, in today's world image is everything.

Your dress code really matters when you meet someone. If you are carrying up yourself in an ordered way, other people will form a good opinion of you. Dressing has the power to change a negative opinion into a positive one. Your dressing will compel them either to give you extraordinary importance or to ignore you completely. It plays a key role in building up trust in the relationship.

I have a friend who I adore. She's a little misunderstood and has a big personality. But what people see when she's coming toward them is a disheveled, frantic-looking, chaotic person.

She's always thrown together, spills all over her top, food on her face and shirt hanging off her shoulder. While I know her heart is pure and she's a kind, genuine soul, after I introduce her to other people, they always leave mouths agape saying "who is that person?" (and not always in a good way.) They don't hear what she's saying. They're too distracted by her physical appearance.

Clothes Set the Tone

Consider that your clothes are a reflection of your personality. They can be a statement. And indication of what you and your business represent. It says "this is who I am" and gives others an idea of who you are. Is what you're wearing reflecting the image you want to give? What's it saying about you and your personal brand? Think about that.

Style Isn't Expensive, Fashion Is

What's important to keep in mind is you don't need to spend a fortune to uncover your style and express that. While designer brands and high-end couture can cost thousands, that isn't what this is about. Style is about expressing who you are.

When you feel great in what you wear, it shows. You hold yourself differently. Carry yourself with my dignity. It projects confidence and assuredness and to your new acquaintance, that shines through.

Be Comfortable

The founder of Amazon, Jeff Bezos has now famously said that "personal brand is what people say about you when you leave the room."

At the end of the day what matters is when you do leave a room, or a meeting or a party... people remember you and you've made a good impression. And remember being comfortable comes mostly from being confident. Openness and confidence combined with a great outfit will ensure people remember you the way you'd want to be remembered.

Body Language... Again

So we touched on body language earlier in the chapter but it's important enough that I'm going to address it again. In more detail.

What Is Body Language?

Body language, though ignored more often, plays a key role in communication. And a huge one at that. We actually use our body to reveal our truest emotions and feelings. It's how we're really feeling expressed through our body. It's actually fascinating once you understand it.

Let's take our gestures, posture and facial expression. When we can "read" these signs, we can take away pretty much everything we need to know. And once we come to understand them, we can use it to our advantage. We see people differently; we understand what they're trying to say and we see how what we're saying affects them. It's also a good barometer to measure yourself in social situations, allowing you to adjust your own body language to come off as more engaging and approachable.

How to Project Proper Body Language?

We know body language is important and when used positively it can add strength to your message. It can bolster a conversation or help relay an idea you have. It helps you avoid sending mixed messages or confusing signals.

How do you project this? Well...

Have an open posture.

Be relaxed, but don't slouch.

Sit or stand keeping an upright posture then put your hands on the sides.

Don't stand with your hands on your hips. It comes off as aggressive.

Have a positive posture. Stand up tall, shoulders back and your arms unfolded and at your sides or in front of you.

Don't be tempted to fidget.

Make eye contact.

Keep Your Hands Visible

Let's expand on this one.

Just like your body language, your hands convey a lot about you. Keep hands visible in a conversation. And keep them marginally active. If you're standing beside someone an occasional touch might be in order. Keep your hands "part" of the conversation, just don't over-do it.

It's also important not to hide your hands by stuffing them in your pockets or folding your arms. Keep them visible to appear more confident.

Smile

We've all been in those situations when we're alone at a party or business function... and someone smiles at you. It seems so silly and random but that smile can make a world of difference in that moment.

It signals that someone found you worthy. Someone projected positive energy your way. You are visible and seen and you've been acknowledged. A smile is a powerful tool.

Not only does smiling make others feel more comfortable around you, it gives you an aura of warmth and openness that invite people your way. People are drawn to a smiler intuitively and it sets you up to invite others to approach. For yourself and others. Smile.

Eye Contact

So many people focus on other areas, that eye contact tends to get skipped. But like the strength of a good handshake or the power of a proper outfit, eye contact can set you apart and tell the world you are open for business.

Maintaining solid eye contact is crucial. In almost all instances, we use our eyes as a communication tool with other people. The other tell-tale sign is we avoid direct eye contact when we have something to hide.

When you are meeting someone for the first time, you don't

have anything to hide. Look the person directly in the eye and don't be the first person to look away.

A Proper Handshake Goes a Long Way

When you are meeting face-to-face and that meeting requires a handshake, the way it plays out says a lot about a person.

Your handshake doesn't need to be a death grip. You aren't the Ultimate Fighting Champion of the World and you have nothing to prove. Think solid versus crushing.

That said you don't want to come off clammy and pasty. Nothing worse than a limp, uninterested handshake. That judgement never leaves you. Literally. So, where's the middle ground?

Make sure both hands are pushed all the way in to meet web-to-web with thumbs facing straight up. Perfect amount of force. Perfect handshake.

Use Your Voice and Tone to Command Respect

Think about some of the most fascinating people you know. The ones people gravitate toward. Chances are if you listen to them speak, they have varied, dynamic intonation.

Any repetitive patterns you make; the same articulation without any variance or interesting inflection, instantly diminishes the power of a conversation. For example, speak in a low monotone with no inference and you'll come off as boring and dull. Add an inflection at the end of each sentence and someone might think you're flaky or immature.

Instead the most interesting and engaging speakers use a variety of tones, inflection and patterns to add a layer of expression to their words. They have more emotion and ultimately connection with their audience.

Now that you have some of these tips and tricks tucked away in your brain, you're probably thinking "great, but now what? I don't know how to even start a conversation with someone." Read on... I have a few ideas that may help you. 66 to be exact.

———————

Takeaway:

- A great first impression is going to make a lasting impression.

- How you present yourself is just as important as what you say.

- Your body language speaks volumes... use it wisely.

Chapter 3

66 Great Conversation Starters to Break the Ice.

"One good conversation can shift the direction of change forever."

- Linda Lambert

A finely composed conversation starter keeps the power to transform a stiff and boring conversation into something juicy and catchy. Tt's something delightful and unexpected.

Once you get the hang of it you see there are few greater pleasures in life than losing yourself in a riveting conversation. When you connect with someone, it can feel like time stands still. The space around you changes and you leave that person feeling alive and energized.

On the flip side, there are few miseries worse than an endless evening of redundant small talk and going around in circles and never getting anywhere. It can leave you exhausted and delated.

I always think really good conversations are like rivers. They flow along running into a few bumps and turns along the way. It takes practice to create a balanced conversation; one that flows naturally and seamlessly. Having a few good questions tucked away can help you navigate slow spots and push past superficial talk.

66 Easy Conversation Topics... you can use to talk to anyone.

So, you can refer back to this anytime. You'll notice most of these are fairly straightforward and ordinary. That's because you don't need to be talking about your beliefs on alien life forms or delve into some obscure philosophy on the misunderstanding of man. Often simple and obvious topics are enough to kick-start a conversation.

1. Tell me about you.

This simply invites someone to tell you something. Invites them to share. They could talk about their job, their kids, their latest vacation. It's a good way to see what's on someone's mind.

2. Working on anything exciting lately?

Great alterative to "what do you do?" Framing the question this way gives the other person an opportunity to share something fun.

3. What's your story?

When you start a conversation this way, you never know where it will lead. It's fun to see where stories come from.

4. What passion project are you working on?

This is one of my personal favorites. Almost everyone on the planet keeps a side hustle to keep himself busy. I like to ask this question to people whom I know from one angle (like say from work) but would love to see what lurks beneath (like say music interests).

5. How do you know the host?

This one can be modified to any event you're at. Chances are if you're both there you have something in common. For work you can say "how long have you worked here?"

6. What was the most important thing of your day?

This can be the best alternative to asking "how are you?" and gets more interesting answers. I use this one a lot with my kids around the dinner table.

7. What was the highlight of your week?

Better than asking "how are you?" or "how's it going?" It also gets someone thinking about an answer instead of defaulting to the autopilot "fine".

8. Have you ever attended to an event similar to this one?

You can tailor this question according to various types of events ranging from birthday parties to marriage parties and networking events.

9. What was the high-point of your day?

An extrovert loves the chance to expand on their story. This question suits best the talkers.

10. Are you going through a busy time?

We are all busy and I don't like to use this one a lot but when someone is distracted or disengaged, I'll throw it in. You can hook them in by acknowledging the fact that they are busy in work.

11. Having fun?

At events I like to look for people that are alone but look like they're having just an ok good time. It's easy to go stand by someone and simply ask "Are you enjoying the time? It can turn out to be a better opener than simply asking "How are you?"

12. What are you doing this weekend?

This conversation starter is always a good one. And if it's early in the week you can rework it to ask "What did you get up to this past weekend?" Sometimes, I also ask "What's your favorite thing to do on the weekend?"

13. What are your favorite restaurants around here?

I love asking people for recommendations. You find out the best tips and discover something you didn't already know.

14. Are you in touch with __sport/tv show/news?

Engaging people with what's going on in the world, is a good way to start a conversation. You get a pulse on who they are and what their interests are.

15. Would you recommend any appetizer or desserts?

Pretty self-explanatory but when you're at an event, ask someone their opinion. Great way to strike up a conversation.

16. What a beautiful/ cool/ ugly/ bizarre venue. Have you been here before?

The one thing you'll always have is context. Regardless of your surrounding there is always something unique to point out.

17. Have you viewed that YouTube video?

That video spread a wildfire over the social media. You can bring into conversation any viral video that has been the talk of the town recently. You can share a hearty laugh if he has seen it. If he has not seen it, you can show them and educate them about it.

18. I'm grabbing a drink/making a coffee. Anyone want one?

This one is great in an office or conference setting. It's a good way to open up further conversation if someone offers to join you on your coffee run.

19. What's the best advice you have received up till now?

If someone shares something with me it's a good follow-up question. It's a nice transition and it yields some captivating topics.

20. Do you have any pet peeves?

This can come up as irritations arise such as... someone is texting at the table, nearby someone is talking way too loudly, the line-up is going to take forever...

Deeper Conversation Starters

Sometimes you want to take things to the next level. Let these inspire you to find a way to connect.

21. While you grew up what had been your dream job?

This is a good one when you know what someone does for a living but you want to see if it aligns with who they thought they'd be.

22. What's your biggest fear?

Whew this one is deep, but so good! It always sparks great conversation.

23. What's your biggest regret?

Talking about regret can open the flood gates and really help you understand someone.

24. Who is your role model?

If you are talking about someone that inspires you (colleague, friend, author, inspiring person) you can lead into asking who their role model is.

Work Conversation Starters

25. Is there a charity you like to support?

It is sometimes better to stop talking about work at all. With the help of this question, you learn about the passions of the other person.

26. I'm a bit nervous about the _____. Have you ever done it before?

You can use this to start a conversation at work with a colleague, to solicit advice on a challenge. Maybe it's a new software platform or a difficult client but when you show vulnerability and ask, you're perceived in a different way.

27. What's the best thing about working here?

Great question to ask co-workers when you're new on the job. And you get to understand the company culture better.

28. Any insider tips working here?

With this one you never know what you're going to get. It's a good one! You get insider tips and build a bond with someone.

First Date

29. What was your dream job when you were a kid?

They might have wanted to be doctor, a racer, a wrestler or a vet. Fun to find out and start a conversation.

30. Pick one. Skydiving. Bungee jumping. Scuba diving.

Great question to see how adventurous your date is. Regardless of how they feel you're going to get a great answer and some insight into your date.

31. What's the most important thing I should know about you?

This question is a great way to get to the heart of the matter. They can share and you can assess.

32. When you were a kid what did you think your life would look like now?

This is a great way to share aspirations and open up about childhood and life.

33. Which of your family members are you most alike?

This question gives you an idea of their family setting but also gives them an easy opportunity to describe themselves simply.

34. Are you working on any personal passion projects?

We mentioned this one earlier but it's a great first-date question. It transitions nicely into extensive discussion about how they spend their time. It's better than the drab "what are your hobbies?"

35. What's the best present you ever gave someone? Ever received?

Awesome question with some pretty terrific answers.

36. What do you want to do non a typical day?

Instead of asking them "What do you do?" you can ask them how they use to spend their day. This gives you a better understanding them.

37. What do you want to do during your vacations?

You may try to ask them what kind of vacations you would

like to have. This results in great conversation and ample "get to know you" responses.

Funny

38. What was your worst fashion disaster?

What makes this conversation starter beneficial is that it crosses the age divide, inviting older members of the group onto center stage to share a fashion faux pas from the past.

39. What's the most embarrassing thing when you were a kid?

It suits well when are in a group, and people have decent time to recall their own story while they are laughing at the story of others.

40. If you are producer of a reality TV show based on your life, what would be the theme song?

This is a good way of talking music without asking pointed "what band do you like" questions.

41. What's your plan for a zombie apocalypse?

Honestly, you'll be astonished by the amount of detail people go into while talking about their elaborate getaway or complicated escape routes. This funny conversation starter can get even funnier picking holes in each other's plans.

Travel

42. What countries have you traveled to?

If you've visited the same place you can share that.

43. What was your biggest "culture shock" in another country?

44. Where in the world would you most want to live? Why?

45. How does your home country compare to here?

(provided they were born elsewhere).

46. What's the worst thing that's happened to you traveling.

It can act as a cautionary tale and can provide for some really funny stories.

47. Have you ever traveled by yourself? (Or you can ask, would they?)

48. Do you speak any other languages?

School

49. What do you study?

Yes, while this seems pretty straight forward it is the simplest way to start a conversation.

50. What's your favorite subject?

51. How do you find the professor's/teacher's approach to learning?

52. How are the other students? Do you get along with most of them?

Networking Event/Happy Hour

Your questions must have a lighter tone.

53. What's keeping you busy lately?

54. Did you come here straight from work?

55. Why did you come here tonight?

56. How long have you lived in this city?

This leads to a myriad of other questions such as where did you live before; do you like it here and what's the best part of the city?

57. If you have the option to eat one food for your whole life, what would it be?

Good when food is involved at an event.

58. What's the last new skill you learned?

59. What did you get done today?

60. I read a written piece that claimed that everyone keeps a side project. Do you agree? Do you have a side project?

61. Are there any skills you thought you'd use in your job that turned out to be unnecessary?

62. What do you think of this venue?

63. You can only attend one type of networking function for the rest of your life. Breakfasts or Happy Hours

64. Do common misconceptions exist about your job?

65. If you could change one specific thing about your job, what would it be?

66. If someone made a movie about your current job, what would the title be?

Feel equipped to head out there and start a conversation? I'm sure some of the above conversation starters will give you some inspiration then next time you're at a cocktail party surrounded by complete strangers.

But before you start a conversation, you'll need to introduce yourself. Yes, another step in meeting someone but not as hard as you might think. Just as important though. I'll explain in the next chapter.

Takeaway:

- Once you get the hang of it you'll realize there are few greater pleasures than a riveting conversation.

- Everyone is in the same boat as you are, so go ahead and break the ice.

- In preparation for going out to any event or gathering, re-read some of the Conversation Starters and keep a list of things you could potentially use.

Chapter 4

How to Introduce Yourself

"A smile is always the best form of introduction."

- Unknown

So, this is a fundamental step in starting a conversation. If you are walking up to someone new or calling someone on the phone, it's the first interaction they are going to have with you. Introducing yourself.

First of all, you need to survey the room and deem what the appropriate level of formality is. Do you go a bit more formal or do you use slang? It entirely depends on the environment.

Staying open and smiling also goes a long way to introducing yourself. Non-verbal cues are typically more telling than the words we use.

Remember:

1. Introducing yourself is much more than saying your name.

2. Your introduction should tell people who you are and it

should encourage people to engage with you.

3. Introduce yourself in a way that make people like and remember you.

How to Introduce Yourself in a Profession Setting?

Make Your Professional Introduction Relevant

You may be a pizza lover, but giving up that information in your introduction is random and useless (unless you're at a culinary convention). Pay attention to the context.

Go Beyond Your Professional Title

In the grand scheme of things your job title is irrelevant. The best way to introduce yourself to someone is to explain what it is you really do. What's your job truly about? Tell them that.

Say What Your Contribution Is

This is related to the previous point. Your professional introduction should tell the other person about how what you do impacts them. What problems do you help them solve?

Be Original

It doesn't mean you have to take the time to write and memorize a hilarious intro. Just take it an extra step. Elaborate on your job. Also, the way you deliver your introduction matters. Remember, a smile can work magic.

Prepare

Not sure how you'll introduce yourself. Ask yourself what you want to be remembered for and craft something around that.

Mind the Cultural Context

As a general rule of thumb just don't offend people. Watch your words, even if you're thinking it, don't say it out loud.

Mind the Funny

Humor is the best ingredient for conversations but you should avoid cracking jokes just for the sake of triggering laughter. More often what appears to be funny to you may not appeal to the listener.

How to Introduce Yourself in a Job Interview

Mind the Context

Suppose the context here is your job interview. During that session, introducing yourself to the interviewer means that you are giving an appropriate answer to the question "tell me about yourself."

Research

This goes to reason. If you're applying you should find out as much as you can about the company. You want to make sure you're a cultural fit. And then you can give a great answer to the question "what are you passionate about?"

Control Your Body Language.

As we've talked a lot about, our body speaks more than we know. During an interview when we introduce ourselves to the recruiter, we have to take care of the following things:

- We must look in the eye of the interviewer.

- We must make sure that handshake is firm.

- Speak with confidence.

- Don't fidget or cross your arms.

Prepare your answer ahead of time.

Come in prepared. You know you're going to have to introduce yourself so think about what you want to say and practice saying it. Now it is time to rehearse what you are planning to say to reduce the chances of awkwardness.

The Best Way to Introduce Yourself – in Any Situation

Be Mindful of the Social Context

I may seem to be repetitive, but this can be top most important thing in a conversation. Your self-introduction ought to stay relevant.

Don't Say Too Much

You must stay away from oversharing irrelevant information. Keep your introduction relevant and useful to the person you're meeting

Acknowledge the Common Denominator

When you include a common denominator it instantly creates connection. When you focus on what you have in common, you'll see how much easier it is to establish rapport.

Listen and Be Present

Listening is a super power. It's not particularly part of the intro but it's the next step. After introducing yourself you'll need to engage in conversation and that can only happen if you're in the present moment listening to the other person.

To re-cap, in almost every situation:

- Be mindful of the context.

- Know your whys and wherefores.

- Resonate with the people around you.

- Focus on what's relevant.

- Don't say too much.

- Prepare.

- Double-check.

How let's change the focus slightly and look at 10 strategies for making a lasting impression... in person.

1. When you are about to greet people in person for the very first time:

This will leave your first impression on the other person. A warm smile is the best way to greet people. Add an introduction to the conversation that includes your first name and last name. Add a welcoming comment. You should try your best to make direct eye contact and keep it for a while. A firm handshake is also very important of your first interaction.

I also think it's great repeating the person's name. For example, saying "It's very nice to meet you David" can go a long way in being remembered.

1. Some people hesitate to tell you their name:

If this happens to you just ask for their name again. Something simple like "sorry I didn't catch your name". Then I would re-state their name (as per the previous point above). This shows them you're interested in them.

2. When a person introduces you to someone but doesn't tell your name:

If someone is introducing you to someone and they don't include your name, chances are they don't know it. Or have forgotten it. So now they can't make a proper introduction. If that happens, offer a warm greeting and make sure to state your first and last name. this shows you were paying attention and you've demonstrated grace.

3. When you have to greet a person, who doesn't remember your name:

When I run into people, I haven't met you for quite some time I always re-introduce myself. "Hi David. It's Joanne Cook. We met at the kid's school."

If I fail to remember the other person's name, I introduce myself by giving my name and hope they respond by sharing theirs. If people don't offer their name I usually say

"Will you kindly remind me of your name?"

4. When you are not introduced:

I was at a concert recently where I ran into an old friend. A moment later his friends stopped to chat for a few minutes. The best way would have been for him to introduce me to his friends. He did not.

When I'm not introduced to people, I usually introduce myself if I get the right opportunity.

5. When you meet a bunch of people you don't know:

We've all been there. Walked into a room occupied by a smaller group of people and stood there awkwardly, not knowing what to do. If you face this kind of situation, you must act proactively and introduce yourself to every person who is present in the room. This will help you stand out from the group. It will also make everyone in the group at ease.

6. When you find yourself in a group of people you are acquainted with:

When you get together with friends or a group of familiar people, friendly greetings should be the order of the day. Then as new people join, be one of the first to offer them a hello. My son Ben calls it "being like a dog". They always show immense happiness on seeing and meeting you. So be a dog.

7. When you are with a group in which some you know and some you are not acquainted with:

When this happens to me, I'll greet the people I know and then start introducing myself to those I don't. There's always a sense of relief in the group when I do this.

8. When you greet a receptionist:

Regardless if it's the receptionist at your car dealership or the office of a high ranking official, introduce yourself with a smile and a greeting. Usually I'll say "Hi my name is Joanne Cook. I have a 2:30 with Lizzie Malo." If I'm in a business situation I'll always hand over my business card along with my verbal acknowledgment.

9. Practice, practice, practice.

Following the above tips will go a long way in helping you make a great first impression. It will also improve existing relationships.

When you implement even some of these, you'll be seen as someone who is confident, friendly and recognizes the value in others. You make them feel comfortable and that doesn't go unnoticed.

Small talk can be the foundation for everything. In the next chapter I'll talk about techniques for navigating it and what to say to initiate small talk.

Takeaway:

- Introducing yourself is far more than stating your name.

- When being introduced to someone, always mind the context. Use relevant data when saying who you are.

- There are nuances in your introduction based on your setting. Know the difference between how to act in a job interview versus a networking event.

Chapter 5:

What to Say? Small Talk Topics and Techniques

"That's all small talk is - a quick way to connect on a human level - which is why it is by no means as irrelevant as the people who are bad at it, insist. In short, it's worth making the effort".

- Lynn Coady

Small talk is, as we've discussed essentially informal conversation. It's used when you're talking to someone you don't know very well either at a party, networking events or some other social gathering.

Below are four strategies we've created to help you with your small talk in any situation.

First, ask open-ended questions.

For a lot of people talking about themselves is their favorite pastime. Not only are we being own favorite subjects but because we know ourselves so well, it's easy to talk about. I mean think about it. Would you have a harder time talking about the quantum metaphysical properties of the moon or your favorite television show. Open-ended questions create an opportunity to have an interesting, dynamic conversation by encouraging the other person to open up a little more.

Second, practice active listening.

It's tempting and sometimes really easy to occasionally tune out (read: please stop talking about your 4 cats and going into detail about how each of their personalities are so distinct). But if you stay present and listening, you'll forge much stronger connections. It doesn't go unnoticed. The other person sees you're paying attention. On the plus side it's much easier to ask relevant and strong follow-up questions and you remember details better if you're paying attention.

Third, put away your phone.

When we're feeling awkward or uncomfortable in social situations it's easy to hide behind our phones. But believe me, nothing will sabotage a conversation quicker than looking at your cell phone. Few people will approach you if your phone is in your face and you send the message that you are not interested.

Fourth, show your enthusiasm.

Small talk might not light you up. It might even feel stressful to you. But if you flip your re-shift your thinking and approach, it just might be fun. Look at it as an opportunity to learn more about other people. You never know who you might meet and what they want to share... so embrace it all.

Keep Things Going

We all see things from our individual viewpoint because we're all a product of our upbringing, our experiences, our narrative and we all subjectively make meaning of the world. The way we see the world is a direct result of some many factors such as our socially constructed background, experiences, culture, education and identity.

Regardless who we're talking with, one thing remains the same. Everyone wants to feel heard.

Usually, asking questions turns out to be the best method for collecting information. You can start by asking some open-ended to engage people into a conversation and understanding the difference between open and close ended questions can go a long way in helping you make conversation and create connection.

More on Open-Ended Questions

First, I'm going to talk about the characteristic of open-ended questions.

1. They require the other person to pause, think, and really reflect on their answer.

2. The answers given usually aren't facts but more so personal feelings, opinions, or ideas about a subject.

3. After you ask the open-ended question, control goes to

the person answering. If the conversation's control stays with the person asking questions (ie – you), you are asking closed-ended questions. This line of questions makes it feel more like an interview or interrogation than a friendly little get-to-know-you conversation.

You Need to Ask Questions That Trigger an Intriguing Story

Ask questions that trigger life stories and prompt someone to share more. Ask about travel to that foreign country or how they want to fund their start-up company or what special talent they have. Inquire about someone's past to draw out a specific story from them.

Choose Positive Questions

You should avoid any kind of political and religious questions to avoid a negative reaction. You need to ask questions that should put the conversation on the right path, giving the other person a chance to think about something he or she is excited about.

Make Sure That Your Questions Make Him or Her Feel Important

The best conversations happen when you want to learn more about a person in terms of their hobbies and occupations. By showing that you want to learn about someone -- even someone who is younger than you – you'll immediately make a positive first impression.

Your Questions Must Build up Momentum.

Ask questions that will build momentum and establish quick rapport with the other person.

11 Questions to Start Conversations

1. Tell me about yourself.

2. What's your story?

(The two non-descript startup questions above let others lead you to who they are what course the conversation will take)

3. What is the source of excitement for you?

4. What can be the most important thing about you that is worth my knowlede?

5. What are you reading nowadays?

6. What is the driving force in your life that keeps you on the edge?

7. What's the best thing that has ever happened to you in the outgoing year?

8. If you could meet one person whom you have not met yet, who would it be? What would you about with that person?

9. When were you the happiest in your whole life?

10. If you have the chance to know the absolute truth to a single question, what question would it be?

11. How can I help you?

Remember Names

We're all guilty of it. You meet someone for the very first time and before the introduction is over you've forgotten their name. Well now it's just too embarrassing to ask again so you just nod and smile and hope someone says it again before the night is over. I've been guilty of that more than once and it's not fun.

Names. More than a word.

What's the most important word in your vocabulary? Your name. It's so important that a lot of times we can't wait for the pause in the introduction so we can tell the other person our name. I'll sometimes even go so far as repeating my name a couple times hoping it will be imprinted in the other's person head.

Mention Their Name. A Lot.

When you meet someone, take the time and effort to learn, remember, and use their name. It goes a long way in making a lasting and positive first impression. When you weave their name into conversation, they are naturally drawn to you and in turn, this will likely cause them to remember your name. This is particularly important in a business setting where trust and confidence are key. Learning another person's name shows respect and goes a long way in building meaningful relationships.

Remembering someone name is a recipe for a win-win. Remembering someone's name makes them feel important and highly valued. That's the secret recipe to win in any situation. You tend to win because they are going to love you because you have made them feel important. They'll also have high respect for you and plenty of admiration for you for making the effort to remember them. From the social and business perspective, remembering names is the most important thing.

Stay Curious in Conversations

Real conversation provides an opportunity for understanding others and understanding real issues that permeate your world. Conversation provides an opportunity to learn. A genuine conversation is more productive for your soul than most other things can be.

One habit that you can create and nurture to enjoy real conversation? Curiosity.

We often think of children or highly creative people when we think of curiosity, yet curiosity should be the cornerstone of a lifelong learner.

Curiosity Makes Us Look for Answers

Asking questions to someone, as we've talked about, is important. But asking too many can feel like an inquisition of sorts. What moves the needle from inquisition to conversation is when we ask but then we take the time to listen. If we're curious about the question, we'll listen to the response.

One of the top reasons that real conversation keeps the power to strengthen realtionships is that real conversation demans active listening that conveys to the other person that you care about them.

Curiosity Makes Us Feel More Interested

Curiosity brings forth interest. I can recall a university class that I flourished in mainly because I figured out the source of my interest. I figured out what intrigued me and I followed that. Once curiosity was provoked, I was infinitely more interested. And once I was interested, good things happened.

Active listening means staying engaged with your conversation partner in a positive way. This means listening attentively while the other person speaks, then paraphrase and reflect back what was said. And here's the tricky part. Do all of that without judgement and offering advice.

Think back to someone you always enjoyed being around. Whether it's a colleague or a family member or someone on your kid's soccer team. Chances are you were drawn to them because they're compelling and really great at listening. They make you feel heard and more than that, they want to hear what you're sharing.

Active listening is about more than mere listening. You have to fully concentrate on what is being said when you are actively listening to people. You need to be attentive with all your senses.

Make Others Feel Important

The essentials of getting people to like you are discernable. Be nice, be considerate, be decent. Those things are all true. However, there are also many smaller, more thoughtful things you can do that have a colossal effect on how others see you.

Ask Questions

Asking other people questions- about their lives, their interests, their passions, will get you extra points. As we've talked about, people are egocentric. They love to talk about themselves. If you get people talking about themselves they'll leave thinking you're the coolest. Even if the conversation wasn't the most stimulating, they are going to like you because you played to their ego.

Sincere Compliments and Plentiful Praise

As noted by the famous self-improvement expert Dale Carneg-ie, individuals crave authentic appreciation. This is in contract to empty flattery, which most people can see right through. No one likes a suck-up, and no one likes being pandered to. What people want is candid appreciation - to be recognized and appreciated for their efforts.

It's also important to be open and extensive with your praise. People love being praised, and what wouldn't they? It feels great to be told you've performed a great job or someone recog-nizes your accomplishments When someone does something right, say so. It won't be forgotten.

Focus on Them and Avoid Interrupting

It's a no-brainer people will like you more if you pay attention and listen to them. This starts with ignoring your social media feed when you're out to dinner, but extends a lot further than that. You can show someone you're listing through body language, eye contact and verbal confirmation.

Since talking about ourselves is just like an addiction, it takes a bit of extra effort to rig of this problem.

You should know whose story is it.

Watch carefully for a story in a piece of conversation. If the story belongs to the other person, don't attempt to hijack the story by start sharing with them your own.

You must search for what you can learn.

I like telling funny stories to friends and family. It is naturally easy to blend in a conversation and start entertaining others. This appears to be fine at times, but you also should learn about the other person as well like what they have been through. Give them time to share what they want to.

It is fine to ask probing questions.

This is considered as a to technique of listening. Just keep asking "What happened next?" If you're doing this, you're giving others time to speak.

When you talk about yourself, keep it short.

If you must share your side of the story, keep it short. Also, add a question to the end of your conversation for the other person to continue the conversation. "This is my experience so what about you?"

Once you get out a few times and start putting into practice some of the things I've touched on so far, you'll start to see how small talk and talking with strangers can be kind of fun. And it's really great when small talk turns into deeper conversation. Next, I'll talk about how to navigate from small talk to bigger talk and how to create connections with almost anyone.

———————

Takeaway:

Understand the importance of open-ended questions and how they're the foundation for deeper connection.

- Remember, the better you are at listening, the better the conversation becomes.

- When you incorporate someone's name into the conversation, you get bonus points and it goes a long way in creating rapport.

- Focus on the other person and cultivate genuine curiosity with every person you meet.

Chapter 6:

Move on to Bigger Talks and Connect with Anyone

"I love those connections that make this big old world feel like a little village."

–Gina Bellman

So, this is where we get around the idea of small talk and cut to the good stuff. Now you're going to hijack that conversation and turn it into something interesting and compelling with your strategic questions coupled with your thoughtful comments.

What you need to do is be interested in the person you're having a conversation with. It's a chance to hear a new story and learn something new. Don't see it as an obligation but more as a potential connection.

- Show enthusiasm

- Smile and make positive gestures often

- Maintain eye contact: Face them and make eye contact

often

• Make your voice tone reflect your interest in the conversation

Here's something to think about. What if we greeted everyone we met with the same level of enthusiasm as we did as if we
were meeting our heroes? Or someone who inspires us? What do
you think about the feelings of the other person if you treated
them with that much enthusiasm?

You'd make a lasting impression because of 3 things.

1 – we like it when someone likes us.

2 – we like people who like us.

3 – we remember those people that make us feel something.

Recently I was at an event that was also attended by a prom-
inent figure in our community. One well known and respected. I
got to sit back and observe this person almost all night. I watched
through the evening as people approached her and here's what
almost all of them did.

They approached her. They initiated and maintained direct
eye contact. They used subtle (and probably unknown to them)
body language, tipping their heads toward her. They held the
handshake for a moment longer (another non-verbal cue saying
it's a privilege to meet you). They smile. Big, genuine, authentic
smiles.

Voice and Relations

We unconsciously receive a message from other people based on tone of voice. This message goes to shaping our opinion of someone. It becomes part of their narrative, part of their 'brand' if you will.

Your tone of voice also implies what kind of relationship you're establishing. If someone is cold and sharp then you can probably figure out they want to establish some distance. On the flip side if they are sweet and warm you can assume they want to get closer. Your tone sets the tone (pun intended) and defines the bond you are establishing with someone.

Current Events Help You Connect

You don't need to be told that social media is an amazing piece of technology. It allows us to stay up-to-date with our friends, family, community happenings and current events. Another benefit? A lot of us turn to social media to get the news. Now we can stay current on every trend, celebrity and event.

When you can reach out to someone about what's going on in their world or the world at large, it can spark conversation and lead to some really interesting back-and-forth. The key is to stay open-minded and be willing to really hear the other person. Sometimes events in the news are triggering and upsetting for some people so try to steer clear of topics that may be controversial or negative.

That said you should also develop your own value and opinions about your life. What do you believe, how do you support that, who are you are your core? Then you can offer an educated and confident opinion when sharing with others.

Read

Books are good for people on so many levels.

When you can share with someone a good book you just read or how the author has impacted your view on a particular subject, it's a beautiful place to start a conversation.

Reading opens your mind up to worlds of fantasy and reality, growth, education, curiosity and fun. All of that combines to make you an interesting person with unique opinions and viewpoints, ready to share at the next dinner party.

Travel

People love to hear comments on how traveling changed them physical and behaviorically. I think I'm way more awesome now than I was pre-travel. In fact, I think travel ups everyone's awesome quotient. Travel always engages us in experiences and reveals truths we didn't know we had. It shows us worlds different from ours and expands our minds, thoughts and feelings.

In my view traveling makes us a nicer human being and way cooler than we were before. We can be way more social than we were before. We learn to make new friends along the way, meet strangers and observe their behavior. Our mannerism is positively affected as we learn to communicate with strangers and make them our friends. Interaction with new people is also boring because it sometimes becomes difficult to kick off a chit-chat. So, it forces you out of the norm and you learn to ask interesting questions that spark great conversation.

What Does Connecting with People Really Mean?

When we refer to connection, we mean more than talking with someone. We've all spent an hour talking with someone we secretly can't stand.

Connection means being open and available to someone else. Vulnerable even. And you get the sense the other person feels the same. To cultivate connection, we need to turn on our empathy and compassion values, which automatically make us happy because we are extending positivity and goodwill when we're connecting.

Examples of human connection are things such as the below:

• having a personal conversation about what is important to you with someone and feeling listened to and understood.

• taking the time to listen to someone else and feeling real empathy for them.

• helping someone else out of unconditional goodwill.

• offering sincere gratitude to another and receiving gratitude from others.

• catching a stranger's eye and both smiling.

Everyone has some sort of fear, even if it is a small one. Maybe you are afraid of speaking in front of people or asking your boss for that raise. You might be afraid to go to rehab for drinking or afraid of telling people no. There are many things you can be fearful of. What do you think will happen when you step outside your comfort zone? What is the worst that could happen? This is how you need to think, if you want to succeed. Fear is great in some situations, but it can also limit you in your life a lot more than you may realize.

Here are a few ways to extend past your comfort zone and get the conversation going.

Ask a Question Related to Your Topic

Intead of start a conversation with a specific topic you should go in warm and start off softly but with intention. You want to prime your partner for what's next. As an example, let's say you're about to open an online store specializing in doggie treats. You start off by saying "so, you a dog person?" Once they answer you can build from there.

Remember the key to leading a conversation where you want is to do so subtly. Forcing a topic is a sure-fire way to annoy them. Once you practice this a bit, you'll get the hang of it.

Ask Open Ended Questions

We've touched on this in previous chapters and will again in future ones but asking open ended questions is a great way to create connection.

Again, these are questions requiring more than simple 'yes' or 'no' answers. They lead your partner to more interesting places with the possibilities of much richer answers.

A simple example is using something like 'What do you think of this event?' instead of 'Do you like this event?' People can expand on their answer and it encourages them to do so.

Make It About the Other Person

Have you met someone who would talk endlessly about something you have no interest? It feels like that they are talking to themselves and you are just one of the audiences. These kinds of people don't understand their listener might not be interested in their talking.

The most effective conversations are the one in which both participants take part. Lots of people are in love with themselves and they would talk about something that matters to them. You can start a productive conversation by asking them valid questions about them like their hobbies or work routine or their eating habit. Food lovers love to talk about what they eat.

Reveal Something Personal

Once you're in the heart of a conversation, people tend to reciprocate to the extent to which you disclose. If someone shares something personal with you, you're more likely to do the same.

In any new relationship, determining the proper amount to disclose can be a tricky thing to determine. Divulge too much and it may seem like you're inappropriate, even desperate. Although... you wait too long and you come off as remote, distant and standoffish.

The Goldilocks principle seems to apply here. You must figure out how to opt for the middle way between revealing too much and too little, based on where in the relationship you are. Follow your gut and trust your internal compass. You'll know when too much is too much.

Just to re-cap and clarify how to make conversations go deeper, create connection and making it meaningful:

1. Warm-Up with Small Talk and Gradually Go Deeper

Jumping into a deep conversation just doesn't happen. Out of the blue connection doesn't really exist. Start first with a few minutes of small talk, get people warmed up and then navigate to more meaningful conversation.

Transition from small talk to deeper connections by asking gradually deeper and deeper questions.

2. Your Environment Should Be Relaxed, Cozy and Intimate

It kind of goes to reason that deep conversations don't mix with high-energy, crowded or loud spaces. Most people are looking for fun or to blow off steam and aren't thinking about deep, meaningful conversation.

Deep conversations are best between only two people or friends who are in the right mood and already are comfortable with each other.

3. Bring up a Subject You're Interested In

Bring up a deep conversation topic loosely related to whatever you're talking about.

Talking about career: Yeah, I think the end goal is finding something that feels meaningful. What's meaningful to you?

Talking about the weather: I think the weather is crappy and I see myself living somewhere tropical and healing. Where do you see yourself eventually? What's important to you in terms of living space?

Sometimes finding a conversation topic isn't the problem. A lot of times our inability to reach out to someone stems from social anxiety and our lack of confidence. I'll touch on that next and give you some practical ways you can overcome your fears and appear confident – even if you aren't.

Takeaway:

- Take control, hijack the conversation and turn it into something you both are excited share.

- Give good thought to your values, interests and what lights you up, so you can express yourself authentically in a conversation.

- We all want human connection and conversation is a great way to fulfil that.

Chapter 7

How to Stop Being Anxious

Our anxiety does not come from thinking about the future,
but from wanting to control it."

- Kahil Gibran

S ocial anxiety is not fun. Basically, it's a fear of being negatively judged and evaluated by people. If you have social
anxiety you worry, you'll embarrass or humiliate yourself
in a crowd and a lot of times you blush, sweat or shake which you
worry about on top of everything.

So, what tends to happen is anxious people avoid social
situations sometimes completely. Any event where judgement
might exist (interview, dinner party, group events, speaking in
public or even being in a crowded room), brings on discomfort
and fear.

It is normal to feel anxious in social situations from time to
time, but it becomes an issue when it gets in the way of your life
and your ability to socialize and enjoy yourself.

You can opt for a number of strategies that can help manage your anxiety and social fears.

- Maintain a good posture

- A confident gesture can make you look and feel really good and it makes you more memorable as well.

- Stand straight

- Avoid slouching when sitting.

- Let your arms hang naturally.

You Should Take up Assertive Posture.

You should opt for standing in an upright and confident position. Your legs must remain perfectly aligned with the shoulders. In addition, keep your feet 4 to 6 inches apart. You are required to distribute your weight equally on the two legs. You need to keep your shoulders moderately back.

This is a posture that projects poise and confidence, not insecurity. It shows that you are open to the person with whom you having communication.

Be Aware of Your Stance

People pick up cues from the position of the person standing in front of them. Even subconsciously we pick up on the non-verbal cue. We know the feet tell us where the mind is at. Someone authentically engaged and aware in the moment will use their whole body in the conversation. They move closer, turn to you and shift their bodies and feet toward you. These signals "I am here and full present."

Have a Memorable Handshake

Handshakes are serious business in our culture. Typically, it's the first time we have physical contact with a stranger. No one forgets a poor handshake. It finds a permanent place in his memory.

In order to intentionally create an equal feeling, the Body Language Dr. offers up a winning strategy from her book's chapter on "Hands, Arms, and Space Consumption." Let's delve into a step-by-step guide:

- You should take a few steps toward a person, making eye contact. Also wear a warm smile on your face. This will signal to that person that you want a handshake.

- Also make sure that your way is not obstructed by a desk or some other solid object. If you are sitting on a chair when the other person enters the room, you should immediately stand up. It is a general rule of a formal handshake that the participants are always standing.

- In a formal handshake your right hand should travel at least halfway into the shared space. The other person will repeat the exercise almost instinctively.

- Bring your palm in a vertical position then slide your hand onto the person's fingers hooking your thumb into the thumb of the other person. Then curl your fingers around the palm of the other person. Both hands will be equally engaged in the handshake.

- You have to decide what should be the level of the grip on the hand. It is natural for smaller people to give a lighter squeeze however bigger people tend to have tougher grips. As a smaller person, you can put on more pressure to complement the hand of your recipient.

- Give five to seven pumps. If you give too many of them, you will be perceived as eager and destructive. If you give too few, you will not be able to enjoy the handshake.

Engage Your Confidence

Nobody is born with boundless self-confidence. We're not Beyoncé. If someone appears to have incredible self-confidence, it's because they've been working at it for years.

Practice imagining an amazing version of yourself. We tend to believe whatever we are always telling ourselves. Affirmations are a great way to give yourself shots of positive and affirming statements.

It takes confidence and guts to ask the big questions of yourself, and even more confidence to put your experience and life out there for the whole world to see. Two people can tell the exact same story with wildly different end results. One captivates, while the other has the audience checking its watch. While we tend to look for exciting stories, the actual story material isn't what separates a good story from a bad one. What makes the difference is the confidence the storyteller puts into their narrative.

Stay Calm, Cool and Collected

We've all found ourselves in the middle of a difficult situation or conversation, whether with a boss, co-worker or even friend or family member.... and we're reminded how easy it is to get riled up.

When we face a difficult conversation and it seems to be slipping out of our hands, we're usually not prepared for what's coming our way. We can feel attacked and naturally we want to fight back. We also know that isn't productive and usually makes things worse.

You Need to Stay Calm

Even though it may feel better in the moment to let yourself go there and get wound up, it's not going to serve you in the end. The more intense the conversation gets, the bigger the explosions and reactions tend to be. No one wins and whatever you're trying to accomplish gets lost.

Then 2 people walk away upset, frustrated and unsettled. When you stay calm you know what happens? You are the one in the ultimate power position. The person that loses their cool is the one that looks silly and ultimately loses out.

If you want to master the art of keeping calm during tough conversations, go through the following three tips that might help you.

Tip #1: Breathe

We hear it all the time but how aware are we? Breathe in,

breathe out. Easy, right?

Breathing has this fascinating consequence of calming your nervous system. Additionally, it gives your mind a focal point; something else to focus on. When your mind is engaged elsewhere there's less chance, you'll saying something regretful.

Tip #2: Posture

Here's another fake it until you make it kind of situation. Even if you aren't feeling confident, be mindful of your posture. A straight back and high head sends a positive message to the other people. It shows you are not going to give up.

Tip #3: Distract Yourself

All we need to do is re-focus our thoughts. Even asking yourself something simple like "what should I make for dinner?" can be enough to temporarily take us out of the situation. Then we can create some distance and stop from obsessing.

Focusing on something small and unrelated to the conversation means you'll be less likely to get caught up in the heat of the moment. Also, when you're distracted it can diminish the hurtful words being slung at you helping you stay calmer and more in control.

Laugh Away...

Research on humor has recently come to light and guess what? It's considered a positive personality trait. Positive psychology which examines what people do well, states humor can be used to make other people feel good, helps in gaining intimacy and is great at buffering stress.

When you can appreciate humor, yourself it says a lot about you too. Humor can easily diffuse a tense situation. Or it can be used to entertain and enlighten. Those that use humor when interacting with others are generally noted as more outgoing, friendly, happier and easier to be around. People flock to funny people. Laughter is a powerful so connection tool. Laughter is useful to form social bonding and is aloa great way to make memories and be likeable.

Think About Something Funny

All of us are surrounded by real-life events that are funny. When you start looking for it, it shows up everywhere. Then when you share one of those real-life experiences framed in a funny and entertaining way, you can lighten up your mood.

Look for an experience or situation that has recently happened in your world and consider a way of marginally exaggerating or remixing the story... just to make a point.

Don't Be in a Hurry to Talk First

One thing I've noticed is people who appear confident don't feel the need to speak all the time. It's like they give off an air of "I've got nothing to prove." Confident people know that good conversation is a two-way street and they pay more attention to the other person because they know this is how they grow and learn.

Instead of seeing it as an opportunity to prove themselves or shine a light on them, they pay attention to the interaction itself knowing it's more enjoyable and gratifying to approach people.

They Let Others Talk About Themselves

Whether we want to admit it or not, we love to talk about ourselves. In fact, we love it so much that it triggers the same sensation of pleasure in our brains as food and money do.

Harvard neuroscientists have concluded that talking about ourselves feels so rewarding we can't help but share our thoughts. When you research the scientific reasoning behind this it makes sense. Talking about our opinions, beliefs and views on the world stimulates the meso-limbic dopamine system. Huh? It's the same chemical associated with the reward and motivation feeling we get from money, food and sex.

The take-away? Want to be confident in conversation while making your conversation partner feel good about themselves (and ultimately you), get them chatting about their interests and their life.

Stop Fidgeting

Fidgeting is an automatic response a lot of people have when thrust in social or potential nerve-wracking situations. Most times we aren't even aware we're doing it; like we're on auto-pilot.

We look nervous when we fidget, shuffle, move around and avoid eye contact. To appear more confident, keep fidgeting to a minimum. Nervous moves take attention away from what you are saying, making it hard for other people to hear what you're saying, because they are instead distracted by your movement.

Keep Cell Phones Away

Using your cell phone during personal interactions can destroy a relationship. When you're talking with someone you shouldn't even glance in the direction of your cell phone. Think about how it makes you feel when it happens to you. If it bothers you (which is does because it sends the signal that you're not important enough) it's going to bother someone else.

If you're expecting a call and your phone rings, you must politely excuse yourself from your company. In no circumstances should you answer your phone in front of anyone.

Same thing with texting. If you're out for a meal or with friends or colleagues, just don't text. It's the equivalent of whispering behind someone's back. You are out with human people so make sure you engage with what's before you. Anything otherwise is considered rude and tactless.

With social anxiety hopefully a thing of the past, or least something you can manage and control now, you are free to head into various situations and create connection with others. Just be aware that you'll encounter people along the way that you don't always jive with or you're quick to label. Next, I'm going to talk about mis-judging people and why you need to see the world from their perspective.

Takeaway:

Where there's a chance of being judged or humiliated, social anxiety can take over and ruin or even prevent you from going out for the evening. Not anymore.

Your confidence is reflected by your body language, your handshake, eye contact and much more. Be aware of all these and try incorporating at least 1 into each conversation. See what it does for you.

Staying calm in the face of a difficult conversation shows confidence and bonus, you remain in the power position.

Chapter 8:

Don't Misjudge Anyone

"Judgment traps you within the limitations of your comparisons. It inhibits freedom."

- Willie Stargell

I think for the most part we all attempt life trying to be open minded and perceiving others without judgement. Despite our best intentions, we're all guilty of judging from time to time.

It might be judgement over little things, like you notice your co-worker extended her lunch break. Or it could be something bigger like you notice a friend acting selfishly and hurtful.

Psychologist and meditation teacher Tara Brach frequently tell a version of this story:

So, you're walking through the woods when you see a small dog. This dog looks cute and friendly and you think nothing of it. As you get closer and try to pet the dog, it snarls and tries to bite you. There goes the warm fuzzies for the dog. No longer does it seems cute and friendly. In fact, now you have fear and maybe a little anger.

As you start to walk away the wind blows a pile of leaves and you suddenly see the dog's leg is caught in a trap. Well now you have context for the behavior and even more interesting you no longer fear the dog. Now you have compassion for it. You now know its aggression was a result of his suffering. Once you see that, it changes how you see a situation.

Based on this story and metaphor, what can we learn? How can we remember this story and become less judgmental?

Don't Blame Yourself

It's how we're wired. As humans our instinctual default is set to survival. Therefore, when you see a dog (or human) who looks like they might bite you (literally or metaphorically) it's only natural you'd feel threatened. Immediately we're thrown into fight-flight-freeze mode and then we can't see the possible underlying reasons for someone else's behavior.

It's a normal reaction – we get defensive and tense. What we need to do is learn to pause before we make decisions or act out when we're in this mode.

Be Mindful

So, like we just said above, judgement is a natural instinct. The key is to catch yourself before you speak up whether face-to-face or through email/text, before you do any harm.

Once they're out there you can't get your words back. So pause. Take a breath. See if you're able to understand where the person may be coming from. Catch yourself and rephrase the discerning and critical thoughts in your head, into something positive. At the very least aim for a neutral one. Go back to the story of the dog in the trap. When we're interacting with others, we really have no clue what the reasons are for their behavior.

Depersonalize

We've all been in a conversation when the other person disagrees with us and we suddenly feel on the defense. When someone disagrees with us, remember it's almost never about you. It's almost always about them. What they're going through, what stuff is in their head, what's happening in their world. It's usually about their internal pain and struggle.

So why not take a step back and give the other person the benefit of the doubt. Go so far as to assume something is going on with them and don't take it personal. Like I said it's not about you. It's about them. Will Smith was quoted as saying: "Never underestimate the pain of a person. In all honesty, everyone is struggling. Some people are better at hiding it than others."

Look for Basic Goodness

This one can take a little practice because we are wired to naturally scan for the negative. Now that you know that, you can practice constantly scanning, re-framing and looking for the good in another person.

Repeat the Mantra, "Just Like Me."

It's a good idea to keep in mind that we are all a lot more alike than we are different. I've found myself in situations where I was internally judging someone until I remembered our oneness. This other person loves their family, just like me. They have dreams and hopes and ideas, just like me. They want to be happy and have a fun life, just like me. And perhaps the most important one? They make mistakes and mess up from time-to-time, just like me.

Reframe

When you see someone, who is doing something you don't like or maybe not the way you would, pause. Pause and maybe think of it as they are simply creating a solution in a different way that wouldn't have occurred to you. When you do this, you become more open-minded and ultimately more accepting of their choices.

The Dalai Lama says" People take different roads seeking fulfillment and happiness. Just because they're not on your road doesn't mean they've gotten lost."

Examine Your Own Behavior

I notice a lot of the time when I'm judging someone, it's because it's triggering something in me. It's highlighting something I don't like about my myself and it's just being mirrored back.

Chances are if we're judging someone, we've been guilty of exhibiting the same behavior. The next time you judge and yell at another driver in traffic, pause and ask yourself "so have I ever driven badly and made a mistake on the road?" Of course, we all have.

Educate Yourself

Another observation I've made is when people are acting out or doing something we'd label as annoying; they might have a hidden disability. And when we take a step back and start to really look at a person and their potential viewpoints, things shift.

For example, if you're at a party and approached by someone with poor social skills, they may have Asperger's syndrome. So, the next time someone invades your personal space (as is common with Asperger's) just remember to not take it personal. It's not about you.

Alberta Einstein said: "Everybody is a genius. But if you judge a fish by its ability to climb a tree, it will live its whole life believing that it is stupid."

Give Benefit of the Doubt

A friend was relaying a story about an incident at work with a co-worker of hers. He was particularly ornery and wasn't the nicest to her. As we were talking, I had the thought that no one wakes up in the morning and thinks "yup, I'm going to a jerk today."

Most of us are doing our best in any given moment. Let's assume that for everyone we encounter.

You Just Do You... and Feel Good About It

This can be beautifully summed up in this Brene Brown quote: "If I feel good about my parenting, I have no interest in judging other people's choices. If I feel good about my body, I don't go around making fun of other people's weight or appearance. We're hard on each other because were using each other as a launching pad out of our own perceived deficiency."

Be Respectful

It's ok to have differing opinions or see the world from an different vantage point but respecting the view, opinions, thoughts and ideas of other people... well it's a critical life skill.

Again, we go back to understanding their choices and seeing their opinions have been formed by their personal experiences, which is vastly and exceedingly different than your own. Therefore, you can't go around telling someone that they're wrong. What's wrong for you often isn't for someone else. Criticizing and telling someone they're wrong is communication suicide.

When you take the time to truly listen and try to understand where the other person is coming from, that's a really admirable character trait. It reflects positively on you but it also expands your capacity to see the world creatively.

Watch the Criticism

When we engage in negative energy and hurl that negativity at another human, you are hurting more than just them. What you put out in the universe comes back to you, so in effect you're hurting yourself too.

You know those people that don't think twice before throwing criticism at someone. When someone presents an idea different from their own, it sparks anger and they become argumentative. There's always going to be difference between us. The key is to remember the differences don't have to be a point of contention. When we criticize no one wins.

Find the Good in Everyone

Everyone you encounter has a personal history and their own unique personal story. That said, we said this earlier in the chapter, we are all a lot more alike than we are different

Like you, they are remarkably precious and beautifully flawed. Each and every time you meet with someone, it's important. It's an opportunity to grow, connect and learn about someone, not unlike you, just trying to figure it all out and making the most of their life.

While sometimes it can be challenging, finding the good in others is such an important part of living a fulfilling, vibrant, fun life. When you see the good in people, they are more likely to see the good in you. You feel more supported, safer and more inspired to be generous and kind.

Well you are almost done this book and should have a pretty good grasp on introductions, confidence, small talk, big talk and everything in between. What's left? One that's often overlooked. How to end a conversation. Just as important as starting one. Read on...

Takeaway:

- As you go through your day and especially when you encounter grumpy people, remember the story of the dog in the trap and remember they have a story too.

- Start depersonalizing comments and things that don't align with you and recognize everyone has an opinion, they are entitled to it and everyone is processing the world through their unique lens.

- Looking for the good in every situation and every person only shines the good in you.

Chapter 9:

10 Ways to End a Conversation Gracefully

"Conversation should touch everything, but should concentrate itself on nothing."

- Oscar Wilde

A lot of this book deals with the art of conversation and how to navigate it. From small talk to approaching the big-ticket items, you have learned how to gain (or fake) confidence, maneuver a conversation and how to be in control. The obvious truth about a conversation is it needs to come to an end.

Sometimes, a conversation goes smoothly and we really enjoy the interaction but when the time comes to end it, we are in a fix.

How to end it is as important as how to start it.

Understanding the nuances of how to end a conversation isn't usually discussed. It's undervalued and under-appreciated but it's just as important as the content itself.

Let's set the scene. You've just been in the throes of a really riveting and interesting conversation with a co-worker or friend. Or on the opposite side of that, image you've just engaged in chit-chat that was tedious and a complete waste of your time. At any rate the conversation is over and you want to move on. The thing is you don't want to seem is rude or uninterested. What should you do?

10 ways to exit a conversation.

1. Say Thank You and Goodbye.

While it might sound simple sometimes the best thing you can do is simply be direct in your approach. "It was really nice talking with you. Thanks for opening up and sharing that experience. I hope you enjoy the rest of your evening." One line that sums it up and signals I'm moving on.

2. Excuse Yourself to Phone Home (Or Something Similar)

This is the good ole I need to make a call exit. You can simply say something such as "Excuse me... I need to call home and check on the kids before they head to bed," or a similar family-related call is a respectable way to exit a conversation. Just make sure when you leave you do in fact make a call. Or at least look like you're making one.

3. Ask who else you should meet.

Asking the person, you're chatting with who else is worth meeting at the party/conference/gathering is a good way not only to engage your current conversationalist but it sets up the exit.

"I told myself that this evening I'd meet 3 new people. Who do you suggest I talk with?" This is a really great way at meeting new people and works well if the person you're talking with is connected to a lot of people at the event. They might even accompany you to someone and make the introduction to get the ball rolling.

If they don't have any suggestions then simply say thank you and move on.

4. Introduce Him to Someone You Know

We're going to flip the last piece of advice. If someone joins your conversation or is close by, take the opportunity to introduce the two. Since you're initiating the new introduction, once it's been done you can excuse yourself and move on.

5. Ask Directions to the Rest Room.

Again, sounds like a simple thing to ask but it's a good excuse and reason to signal the conversation is over. Just like the phone call home, make sure when you walk away you head to the rest room and not directly to someone else or to the bar. This saves embarrassment and avoids misunderstandings or offense.

6. Offer to Deliver a Drink.

This is a strategy I've used a lot in my life. When the conversation seems to be shutting down, I will say something like "I'm heading over to grab a drink (or coffee or whatever). Anyone want anything?"

Most times that question is met with a polite refusal but if they take you up on the offer, it's quite respectful to grab the drink, deliver it and say something along the lines of "I really enjoyed meeting you. Enjoy your evening."

7. Ask If You Will Meet the Other Person at a Future Event.

To wind things up you can project to the future and ask about potential events. "I've really enjoyed connecting with you today. Will you be at the next event? Perhaps we can continue our conversation then." This lets the other person know you've enjoyed chatting and it also leaves the door open for future connections. But for this purpose, it signals you are moving on for now.

8. Ask for the Other Person's Card.

Sounds simple and maybe a little too easy but sometimes the most obvious approach is the easiest. Ask for their card, look at it for a moment then thank them for their time.

9. Give the Other Person Your Card.

Grabbing your own business card and handing it off is the reverse of the point above. Saying something like "here's my card. Please contact me if I can help in anyway."

If you're not interested in their card or they don't offer you one, suggest yours instead. It's a pretty sure-fire signal that the conversation is ending.

10. Plan a Get-Together.

If you and the other person really hit it off and you'd love to carry on with the conversation, ask them to meet for coffee down the road. Then you will have an opportunity to talk and be a bit more intimate in your discussion. It also means you have the anticipation of carrying on in the future while still having the time to find other interesting people to chat with in the moment.

Bonus: Ask to Connect on Social Media.

There have been times I'd like to follow up with people on social media. Whether I want to stay connected or am interested in learning more about the person, I'll ask to connect on social media.

Say to them something like this "thanks for your time. Can I connect with you on LinkedIn?" I typically like to ask for approval before reaching out before sending a request but that's not a hard and fast rule.

Conversation Enders/Exit Lines

Here is a rundown of the ways I use to end a conversation. They are considerate, graceful one-liners you can use anytime you want to leave a conversation. If the situation warrants, be sure to pair your one-liner with an endearing smile and a handshake.

#1: Wish you wonderful moments with your weekend plans.

#2: Please keep my business card. It was a pleasure to meet you.

#3: It was an amazing experience to talk to you.

#4: I wish you good luck on the start of your new project.

#5: It was fun talking with you. I'll pop you an email.

#6: I'm going to get a drink … it's been a pleasure.

#7: I'm really glad we met. Thanks for sharing that story.

#8: Great discussion with you.

#9: Can I have your business card for future correspondence?

End with appreciation. Whatever methods you use to end a conversation, it's always nice to end it with appreciation. Small talk expert Debra Fine calls appreciation "a compliment with closure."

Re-cap what you talked about, thank them for their time or for sharing their experience with you or simply say it was fun getting to know you. Whatever you say, make sure it's sincere and only say it if you truly mean it. As a bonus, use their name too. It builds one last bit of rapport with the other person.

Takeaway:

- Ending a conversation is just as impactful and important as how you start one.

- Be respectful and gracious regardless who you're talking with.

- When you end with appreciation, it won't go unnoticed.

Conclusion

Social cognition means how we understand people. This enables us to predict how they will behave and how they will share certain experiences. In addition, it is also critical that we understand certain nuances in everyday speech to make out the hidden verbal cues in the speeches of our colleagues and bosses. Many a time people don't mean what they say and don't say what they actually mean. For example, when someone says, "it is getting cold." It indirectly means that you should go and close the window or the door. You can easily understand the hidden meaning in the remark.

Practice makes us understand what is running in the minds of people, even if they don't speak it out. This is how we can understand their beliefs, experiences and feelings. When we place ourselves in others' shoes, we tend to learn how they think and will behave in a certain situation. This is the start of our understanding of our colleagues and family members.

Reading people is complex. Have you ever had a look at a person and figured out how that person thought or what his nature was? Did you reach the right conclusion? Or did you make a mistake right from the start? The conclusion doesn't matter. What matters is that you tried to make a judgment. If you are always right about your judgment, you are a lucky person because there are so many people in the world who have to go through lots of reading and practice sessions to be able to read other people perfectly. You always need this skill, whether you are an executive in a company who has to run a team of a hundred people or an employee who has to do lots of work and keep his boss happy. The need for reading people increases when you change a job or meet a new boss. Only after a careful judgment of that person, you are able to better communicate with them.

Similarly, at home, you have to read the mood of your father and mother, especially when you have to communicate something important such as your marriage proposal, some girl or boy you like or about the future of work. Only when they are in a good mood, you can be able to say and be heard positively what you want to say. Perhaps you have scratched their favorite car so you will have to catch them in the right mood to communicate that tragic news to them. If you misread them, you will land yourself in great trouble.

Reading people is important and there is more than one reason for that to prove that this is a good skill to add to your skillset. Now that you have gone through the book, you can understand that reading people is essential before you approach a person to talk to him or her. If that person looks friendly, you can go on and open your heart to him; otherwise, you may decide to hold your feelings a bit longer. This skill can enable you to judge if your friend is upset. You can go on to know the reason of his disturbance and help him accordingly. If you are a master of reading and analyzing people, you are very well on the road to success at your workplace. You have to meet people who have different types of behavior. If you misjudge a cunning person and tell him your secrets, you have brought doom to your life by your hands. Similarly, if you have misjudged a sincere person and kept him at bay, you are missing out on a pure friendship that could have helped you climb the ladder at your workplace.

In addition, if you have to gain expertise in the skill of reading people, you are well on your way to be a social magnet. You can easily read people and judge the situation and tailor your communication accordingly. That's how you can win lots of friends and get popular in your social circles. For example, if people appear to be friendlier, you can approach them with a smile on your face and informal greetings. Otherwise, you can take up a formal persona and deal with them accordingly. So, reading people helps you take up a fluid personality that you can shape up according to the expectations of those around you.

This is a general rule. When you say things that others want to hear or behave as others expect you to do, you become a popular figure in your circles because you have mastered the art of keeping them in comfort zones those near you. Your social circles will remain full to the brim always. Understanding the feelings of others is an art that helps you anticipate what is running in their minds, which can help you tailor your speech.

The world is full of confusion. Misreading people leads to a flawed judgment that in turn leads to an inaccurate assessment. Sometimes, a misread facial expression can lead to cracks in the relationship and cause the death of it. For example, she loves you but just doesn't want to talk to you because she had a bad day at work, but you misread her facial expression and distance yourself from her. No matter how nicely she explains her position to you until you read it yourself, the element of doubt will remain in your mind. This small element can plague the entire relationship in the days to come.

So, reading people plays a crucial role in shaping up your intimate relationship. In addition, it can help you at your workplace. This book has walked you through the methods you can use to read people. These methods include reading people with the help of understanding their body language like the movement of their hands and arms, how they sit or how they walk. I have also explained in the book how you can read the facial expressions of a person to judge what he is thinking or what he has to say to you. You can read people by some pretty micro facial expressions to better your judgment of them.

A chapter in the book explained different types of people and different personalities that people take up to move through this life so that you have a better know-how of which type of personalities exist and what is the mindset that is linked to each personality. This will help you better judge people when you are able to identify them with a personality that you have read and integrated into your brain; the process of reading them gets smooth and easy. You also learned about the gut feeling and how it plays a crucial role in guiding your decision-making in day-to-day activities. In addition, you learned about the human vibe and how it can be linked to reading people. How you can study emotional energy and know how the other person makes you feel when he is close to you and how is he going to deal with you and whether you should keep in contact with him or not for the long term.

The book also explained different types of liars like what are their types and how they are you can deal with them. What steps you should avoid and what steps you must take to tackle them. You have learned the adverse effects of mixed signals if you misread them. Mixed signals have ruined lots of relationships and it continues to do so, just because we lack skills in sorting them out, and we always make a hasty decision.

I hope you have learned a lot and have started sorting out things in your brain. We have the basics of reading people in our subconscious. All we need is to sort it out by studying what a typical reaction means and then start implementing it on our social interactions.